"Muller insightfully reveals the stories both large and small that divide and unite their readers, and profiles the dedicated individuals who even risk their lives to bring controversial issues and facts to light."—*Booklist*

"[An] engaging account of local journalism outside the major urban hubs. Without the muscle of a big-city newspaper—or the benefit of working at arm's length from public officials and advertisers—the passionate lunatics who put out America's small-town weeklies labor to keep local politicians honest while coping with anger, threats, pleading, exhaustion, poverty and, often, instead of gratitude, cold shoulders from neighbors on the checkout line at the IGA."—*Wall Street Journal*

"*Emus Loose in Egnar* is what Mark Twain might have written if he had taken better care of himself and lived long enough to meet the collection of loners and lunatics in this book. I laughed until I cried, because I have been there." —Richard Reeves, author of *Daring Young Men* and the founding editor of the *Phillipsburg (NJ) Free Press*

"[Muller's] findings make fascinating reading."—*Los Altos Town Crier*

"Muller makes us glad for the 'hyperlocal' stalwarts who do things right." —*Online Journalism Review*

"A read through this rather gentle, inquisitive look at small-town weekly newspapers could be beneficial to your health. It may even lower your big city blood pressure."—*New York Journal of Books*

EMUS LOOSE IN EGNAR

Emus Loose in Egnar

Big Stories from Small Towns

JUDY MULLER

UNIVERSITY OF NEBRASKA PRESS | LINCOLN AND LONDON

© 2011 by the Board of Regents
of the University of Nebraska
All rights reserved
Manufactured in the United
States of America

Library of Congress Cataloging-
in-Publication Data
Muller, Judy.
Emus loose in Egnar:
big stories from small towns / Judy Muller.
p.   cm.
Includes bibliographical references.
ISBN 978-0-8032-3016-3 (cloth: alk. paper)
ISBN 978-0-8032-4374-3 (paper: alk. paper)
1. Community newspapers—United States.
2. Journalism, Regional—United States.
3. Reporters and reporting—United States.
I. Title.
PN4784.C73M85 2011
071'.3—dc22   2010051804

Set in Scala by Bob Reitz.
Designed by Nathan Putens.

For my students

CONTENTS

Acknowledgments ix

Prologue 1

1 Everything Old Is New Again 11

2 Crusaders 31

3 Curmudgeons 61

4 Too Close for Comfort 91

5 This Town Isn't Big Enough
  for the Two of Us 113

6 All the Names Unfit to Print 155

7 Never Speak Ill of the Dead 173

8 School Sports: Holy Hyperbole! 193

9 They Don't Make 'Em Like
  That Anymore 207

10 Coming Home 231

Bibliography 245

ACKNOWLEDGMENTS

Without the expert guidance of Al Cross of the Institute for Rural Journalism and Community Issues at the University of Kentucky, I would never have known where to begin this journey. He pointed me in the direction of the editor of the *Canadian Record* in Texas, Laurie Ezzell Brown, whose courage and passion continue to inspire me. Laurie and her staff went out of their way to make me feel welcome in Canadian, even as they hustled to get out that week's paper. Over the last two years, I have encountered the same grace under pressure from editors all over the country; taking the time to talk about themselves and their work while trying to *do* their work was no easy task.

And so I want to thank all those who gave so graciously of their very valuable time: Jason Miller, M. E. Sprengelmeyer, Ben Gish, Bill Bishop, Tom Bethell, Bruce Anderson, Mark Scaramella, Jim Stiles, Adrien Taylor, Bill Boyle, Linda and Doug Funk, Wes Eben, Michael Dillin, Jim Eshleman, Scott Russell, Ben Cloud, Joe Fitzpatrick, Denny McAuliffe, Rebecca Convery, Brett Thomas-DeJongh, Alex DeMarban, George Ledbetter, Kevin Bersett, Benjy Hamm, Tonda Rush, Shannon Smithey, Heather Lende, Homer Marcum, Bob Beer, Marta Tarbell, Andrew Mirrington, Ellen Metrick, and Deb Dion.

I am also grateful to my friends in Norwood: Charlie Bausch, who discovered all those yellowing copies of the *Norwood Post* while renovating an old house; the owners of various establishments, including the Happy Belly Deli and Two Candles, for providing a warm and appetizing space for conversation and writing; John and Susie Mansfield for the kind of honesty and humor only family can provide (and get away with); Grace Herndon, who—right up until her death in 2009—wrote passionate, beautifully crafted columns for newspapers in Telluride and Norwood about whatever interested her at the time, which was damn near everything; and Susan, Cynthia, Leslie, Karen, and my other pals in town who have embraced this Californian as a true Norwoodian.

Thanks to my colleagues at the University of Southern California's Annenberg School for all their encouragement, to Randi Murray for her early efforts in shaping the proposal, to my friend and fellow journalist Margot Roosevelt for saying, on a hike long ago, "What a great idea for a book!" when I first spoke about this out loud, and to Heather Lundine, Chris Steinke, Ann Baker, and Bridget Barry at the University of Nebraska Press for their astute editorial guidance.

I owe a huge debt of gratitude to Martha Bardach, my friend and outstanding photo editor, for helping me compile the images for the book.

Finally, my love and gratitude to my daughters, Kristen and Kerry, for their unwavering confidence in my abilities, even when I have my own doubts. And to my students, who remind me why I am doing this in the first place.

Prologue

This just in: *journalism is not dead*. It is alive and kicking in
small towns all across America thanks to the editors of weekly
newspapers who, for very little money and a fair amount of
aggravation, keep on telling it like it is. Sometimes they tell it
gently, in code only the locals can understand. After all, they
have to live there, too. But telling it like it is also takes courage,
as one tenacious editor in the Texas Panhandle discovered. Her
coverage of politics and crime (and the convergence of the two)
prompted some readers to express their "editorial opinions"
with rocks and bullets. Like many of the gutsier publications,
her paper is a stand-tough, family-owned operation.

That commitment to compassionate and courageous storytelling is good news for those of us—reporters and readers
alike—who had begun to despair over the health of the First
Amendment in this country. The profession that won my heart so
many years ago (when I started, as so many of us do, by reporting for a paper in a small town) is experiencing a wrenching
and revolutionary transition. The Internet and the blogosphere,
twenty-four-hour cable television and TIVO, iPhones and iPads,

podcasts and God-knows-what-next-casts—this competition has threatened the so-called mainstream media, splintering the audience and advertisers and prompting publishers and network execs to do what they do best: cut costs. "Costs" is bean counter–speak for "people," as in: the people who do the reporting. Just how eliminating journalists is supposed to make for a better journalistic product is puzzling, but this book is not about those issues. After all, by the time this work is published (in the old-fashioned way we have come to understand the word), the debate over how to "monetize" journalism will no doubt have traveled, at warp speed, to frontiers we have yet to imagine.

This book is about a different kind of bottom line, one that lives in the hearts of weekly newspaper editors and reporters who keep churning out news for the corniest of reasons—the belief that our freedoms depend on it. Not that they would necessarily express it that way. As the editor of the paper in Dove Creek, Colorado, put it, "If we found a political official misusing taxpayer funds, we wouldn't hesitate to nail him to a stump."

You can find these brave people in the newsrooms of small towns all across America. I know because I spent more than a year tracking some of them down. And what I discovered was that many small town papers are thriving, mostly because absolutely no one else does what they do: document the births, deaths, crimes, sports, local shenanigans, and many other events that only matter to the 2,000 or so souls in their circulation area. Taken together, however, these "little" stories create a mosaic of American life that tells us a great deal about who we are—what moves us, angers us, amuses us. As a weekly editor in Alaska said, "I feel as though I am writing the Great American Novel, one week at a time."

My fondness for small-town weekly newspapers is clearly rooted in my fondness for small towns. It's pretty tough to appreciate one without the other, actually. And appreciation is in the details, something I have learned firsthand.

Some years ago, I built a house in Norwood, Colorado, a small town in the mountains of the southwest part of the state, some twenty-five miles downriver from the more famous ski resort town of Telluride. My brother, John, has lived in the area for decades. He and his wife Susie left Telluride and settled in Norwood (or "The Wood of Nor," as Susie fondly calls it) in search of the small-town ambience that once defined Telluride. Norwood, population 500, elevation 7,100 feet, is the kind of town where everything is only "a few blocks over that way," including the Splish Splash Buggy Bath, where you can get your car washed for less than three dollars. Or the dry cleaners, where asking for a receipt is considered an insult. Or the tiny post office, where a sign was once taped to the door that read: "To the Garden Hose Thief: It takes a real low-life to steal both the hose and the geraniums. Please return the hose, at least, and no questions will be asked."

It's the kind of town that boasts several outstanding chefs, including one known simply as "Chef" who serves up superb meals at the Lone Cone Saloon, an establishment named for the Mount Fuji–like peak that serves as the town's dramatic backdrop. Out-of-towners who stop at the Lone Cone for a quick bite en route to more famous destinations are often astonished to receive delicately prepared salmon with fresh vegetables steamed to al dente perfection. Also astonishing are the homemade soups served up at Two Candles, a combination restaurant, antique store, art studio, and microbrewery. A local painter by the name of Ziggy creates large canvases there depicting, among other things, mythical creatures whose faces sometimes resemble local citizens. "Ziggy can paint anything," one patron told me, in unabashed admiration of the sheer quantity of the Ziggy oeuvre. The Hitchin' Post Cowboy Bar, on the other hand, is not known for its oeuvre, cultural or culinary. It is known for drinking, dancing, and fighting. A counterpoint, if you will, to trendiness. As marketing strategies go (though I doubt the term has ever been uttered at the Hitchin' Post), this approach is shrewd. Consider the case of the guy who moved to Norwood from a resort town in another state, bought a popular local restaurant, and promptly changed the menu to make it sound more upscale. Everything from cinnamon rolls to scrambled eggs received a fancy title. No one could understand the menu, and they resented having to ask. A once-thriving business went under in a matter of months, in part because of the Norwoodian disdain for putting on airs.

And then there is the Happy Belly Deli, the geographic and gastronomic center for morning commuters. It inherited (and managed to maintain) the reputation of its earlier incarnation, Karen's Express. Karen LeQuay was an institution in Norwood gourmet circles (granted, a very small circle) until she finally tired of working and decided to sell her business. A pity, I thought at the time, because it took me awhile to win acceptance at this little café in the middle of town, the unofficial gathering place for everyone on their way to work. In the best Seinfeld tradition, Karen was the Soup Nazi of Norwood. She did not suffer fools. It took me a very long time to earn a smile and a bit of conversation. I have no idea what broke the ice, but I knew it had melted when Karen asked if I would like to be a judge for the county fair's pie contest. I leaped at the chance (groveled, really) only to realize later that I had been on a sugar-free diet for months and that such an event could blow every brain cell I had left. But I bravely sat down with several other judges at a long table in the school gym and accepted the challenge. "Sugar high" does not begin to describe the manic binge and hangover connected to sampling some twenty pies in quick succession. No matter, I told myself. I had been officially welcomed into the Norwood family. Lemon meringue had never tasted so sweet. (That would be Betty Greager's lemon meringue, which wins almost every year, something I wish I had known before wolfing down enormous forkfuls of lard and sugar in an attempt to be fair.)

Norwood is a tiny town with a grand view. It sits atop a sunny mesa of ranchland set against a backdrop of breathtaking mountains, jagged peaks that hold their snow well into the summer. Norwood also provides a few cosmopolitan touches not always found in small ranching communities. The Uptown Salon ("uptown" surely an ironic reflection on the fact that the entire main drag is only a few blocks long) offers facials, manicures, and massages that rival any pricey spa in Telluride. And small wonder: many of the people who work at those pricey spas live in Norwood. At one point, there were also two yoga classes for local women who came as much to mingle as to meditate.

Living in a small town obviously has its drawbacks, of course. Calling repairmen listed in the yellow pages does no good. They always live somewhere else, like Telluride. And they always say, "Norwood? I don't go there." So when I needed a plumber, I went over to Karen's for a reference.

"That would be Grizz," said Karen.

"Grizz what?"

"Just Grizz. When you see him, you'll understand."

"Oh. And how would I get in touch with Grizz?"

"You can't."

Seems Grizz doesn't plumb for just anyone. He works only for friends, a much higher category than pie judge.

I finally managed to track down a former plumber, a man who liked a drink or two but was really fabulous, I was assured, if you could catch him early in the day. I did. Even then, it helped that I was introduced as "John's sister." Norwood is the only place on earth where I am always introduced this way. At first I resented it, but I soon learned to see it as a plus: not only did it help me secure plumbers when I needed them, it also allowed me to avoid being branded as one of those outsiders who "Californicate" Colorado by building second homes in communities where they have little or no involvement. Or, perhaps, too much involvement.

The importance of having kin in Norwood first hit me when I was sitting in my office at ABC News in Los Angeles in 2004. A desk assistant called me and said, "An item is running on the AP Wire that sounds like your town in Colorado. Norwood, right?"

Right. Seems someone had leaked a local story to the Associated Press about a flap over *Bless Me, Ultima,* the critically acclaimed book by Chicano author Rudolfo Anaya. An English teacher had assigned the book to a class at Norwood's high school (typical graduating class: 12). An outraged parent, a member of a conservative Christian church, thought that the book contained inappropriate language and pagan values. The school superintendent, Bob Conder, responded by gathering all copies of the book and handing them over to the parent for disposal in the town dump. He did this, by the way, without ever talking to the teacher, the other parents, or the students themselves. In fact, he never even read the book. Nevertheless, he told the AP, "That's not the kind of garbage I want to sponsor at this high school."

BIG mistake.

Book burnings, or any variation on that theme, always make for good copy, and this was no exception. Especially when it came out that the book, about a Latino teenager in New Mexico struggling to reconcile his religious upbringing with his emerging independence, had won numerous awards and was on Laura Bush's suggested reading list for young people. I don't know if she ever learned of this case, but as a former school librarian, she might have been aware that *Bless Me, Ultima* was on the American Library Association's list of the hundred most frequently challenged books in the United States, along with other mind-rotting, filthy stuff like *Huckleberry Finn* and *All the King's Men*.

While most of these details were included in the AP story, the local paper, the *Norwood Post*, had also been all over it. Letters to the editor protesting the superintendent's decision poured in. Well, they actually trickled in, but in a town where people are reluctant to put in print opinions expressed quite openly at, say, the Lone Cone Saloon, a trickle is a comparative flood. When the students decided to stage a sit-in protest (there's nothing like telling teenagers they can't read something to make it suddenly attractive), *Post* editor Margo Roberts brought them pizza. Talk about access. Certainly better than I had, calling as a network news correspondent from Los Angeles. But call I did, asking to speak to the school superintendent.

Conder answered the phone with a curt "I'm not talking to any more reporters," adding, "I am only talking to you because you're John's sister." He told me that he regretted acting so hastily, that he had personally apologized to the students, and that he had even offered to buy more copies of the book with his own money. As far as he was concerned (and desperately hoped), the story was over.

And it was over, at least at the national level. The mainstream media, let's face it, are not big on follow-up or follow-through. Fortunately, when sheer tenacity and endurance are required, local weeklies pick up the slack. The *Norwood Post* was on the case. And months later, when the same superintendent tried to persuade the school board to fire the teacher involved despite her excellent evaluations, the paper alerted its readers. Half the town turned out for that school board meeting, and I witnessed a string of passionate testimonials from parents and students who lined up to praise the teacher. They recognized a backdoor backlash and were having none of it. At the same meeting, there were also a few parents who were still insisting that the board require the teaching of "decent Christian values"—an interesting take, I thought, on the separation of church and state. The board members, feeling the heat of the majority and suddenly made aware that they were, in fact, elected officials, rejected the superintendent's recommendation not to renew the teacher's contract. Instead, Conder was the one who would soon leave his position.

The last time I dropped by the Norwood school, I spotted *Bless Me, Ultima* sitting on a shelf in the middle of the library under the sign "Recommended Reading."

If you want an example of the First Amendment in action, of citizens making sure their voices are heard, of young people taking an interest in something bigger than themselves, the Norwood book banning incident is a pretty good place to start. And without the spotlight of the local newspaper, which was the first and—more importantly—the last to report it, the outcome might have been very different.

With Norwood as my touchstone, I set out on a search for other big stories from small towns, looking to plumb the depths, and the shallows, of small-town journalism. Whether the stories are about banned books or escaped emus, they serve to inspire and amuse and transport us to Britney-free zones across America, where celebrity journalism amounts to the crowning of this year's homecoming queen and "citizen journalism" flourishes as club news, guest columns, and, most frequently, obituaries. "We let folks write about their own loved ones," says one editor, adding that "even if everyone in town knew the deceased was a son of a bitch," his passing is no time to rob the family of one last moment of spin control. Besides, all those glowing adjectives fill up a lot of space.

Come along, then, on a grassroots tour of small-town journalism, where putting everything on the line in the name of truth can have life-altering consequences.

Not to mention a few laughs.

CHAPTER ONE

Everything Old Is New Again

With all the hand-wringing about the "death of journalism," it is more than a little ironic that small-town papers have been thriving by practicing what the mainstream media are now preaching. "Hyper-localism," "Citizen Journalism," "Advocacy Journalism"—these are some of the latest buzzwords of the profession. But the concepts, without the fancy names, have been around for ages in small-town newspapers. And the weeklies have learned a lesson from watching the financial stress of their city cousins: don't give it away. Most of the weeklies have discovered that people are still willing to pay not only for something they can hold in their hands, something they can clip and file in the family scrapbook, but also for content on the Web, especially if they cannot get that news anywhere else.

And so far, anyway, they can't.

When I started this journey, a veteran journalist from a major daily paper said, "Better hurry, or there won't be anyone out there left to interview." But I found the opposite to be true. There are some eight thousand weeklies in the United States, and most of them are doing quite well, thank you very much, thanks to an endless source of material (i.e. life in a small town) that local readers crave, not to mention advertising that local merchants are willing to buy to reach their "target" audience (i.e. their neighbors).

When I toss out some of the circulation and profit figures for weeklies as a rejoinder to the mainstream media naysayers, they invariably counter with, "Well, they're bound to die out eventually, once the older generation retires," as though small-town journalism is a quaint piece of Americana destined to fade away.

Not so.

As exhibit A, I offer up Jason Miller, who decided to start a local newspaper last year in the town of Concrete, Washington, in the heart of the Cascade Mountains.

That's right. I said "start."

The *Seattle Times* heralded the development with this tongue-in-cheek lead: "CONCRETE, Skagit County—Shocker story—Man plans to start a newspaper here! He doesn't believe it's over for print. Another shocker: businesses in this small town of 850 also still believe in print . . . and say they will advertise. And locals say they'll subscribe."

I had to see for myself. When I asked Miller if I might visit him in Concrete, he responded with an invitation of his own. "Can you come during 'Cascade Days?'" he asked, "and be part of my parade float?"

And so I found myself walking down the main street of this very small Northwest town alongside Miller's *Concrete Herald* "float" (his car towing a trailer full of newspapers) with three local kids, news delivery bags slung over our shoulders, tossing rolled-up issues to the crowd. You would have thought we were tossing out hundred-dollar bills. Many in the crowd cheered and stretched out their hands for extra copies. More than a dozen people along the four-block parade route shouted "THANK YOU!" to the grinning young editor. One woman ran up to the car, decorated in the paper's logo, and vigorously shook Miller's hand, tears in her eyes.

I am not making this up.

We did not win the award for best float (notice how I have lost all journalistic objectivity?). That honor went to the Redneck Laundromat, which featured a giant cake on top of the car in honor of Concrete's centennial celebration ("Cementing the Future for a Hundred Years").

Nevertheless, I had witnessed an amazing outpouring of gratitude to a young man who was willing to bring back something concrete to Concrete and other tiny towns along Highway 20, something they had lost back in 1991, when the original *Concrete Herald* folded after ninety years of publishing. "When it went out of print," said Miller, "the communities started to fragment, between themselves and amongst themselves." The area, he could see, needed some kind of "connective tissue." A former publisher, Anne Bussiere, told him something that he thought at first was hyperbole. "When the *Concrete Herald* folded," she said, "the community crumbled." Now he believes her.

After all, this small town in the Cascade Mountains is isolated in a number of ways. The only daily paper in the region—the *Skagit Valley Herald*, or svH—rarely bothers to send a reporter to cover local events in the string of towns (including Concrete) that line the North Cascades Highway. Almost everyone I spoke with—from the towns of Lyman, Sedro-Wooley, Marblemount, and, of course, Concrete—complained about the coverage, or lack thereof, by the svH.

"You don't really get the flavor of this town from the svH," Chuck Trueman told me. I met Chuck and his wife Norma while watching a chain saw competition at the Cascade Days festivities. The Truemans are both volunteer firefighters in nearby Lyman, and Chuck's family has been farming in the area since the 1880s. "Concrete," he said, "is different from Sedro-Wooley just down the road. The farther up the highway you go, the more isolated these mountain towns are. And there are so many stories to cover," he adds, "about old, established families and all the new people. Who are they, what are their unique stories?"

As we spoke, I was transfixed by what appeared to be a unique story unfolding in front of us. The most famous competitor in the Hopped-Up Chain Saw Division had just walked onto the field. Lee Williamson, I was told, made custom chain saws for a living. He had just reverentially lifted one of these gleaming behemoths, a "hopped-up" design complete with an enormous exhaust pipe, out of the back of his pickup truck. Williamson looked like a character John Goodman would play in a Coen Brothers movie: a huge man with shocking red hair, a face to match, and a few fingers missing (not unusual in logging country, I was told). Williamson strode toward his target—a large log brought in for this event—wearing leather chaps and a determined expression. He whipped out a small brush and carefully swept away the dirt on the part of the huge log he was planning to cut. When the winning time comes down to tenths of a second, apparently every speck of dust matters. Then he took out a marker and drew a line along the top of the log. No other chain-saw competitor had done all this, and the crowd was now giving him its full attention. After a roar of the chain saw and a "go" from the judge, Williamson sliced down through the thick log and then back up, carving out a slice as neat and clean as a piece of deli ham. Only this was a very thick piece of solid wood, and he managed to do it in 7.16 seconds. No one else came close.

Surely, I thought, this guy would make for a great profile in the newspaper? Not really, Miller told me. Williamson was from another area, a well-known pro who traveled to competitions around the state. "Besides, he's been done," Miller explained. Instead, he said, he was eager to tell stories about the locals. And he believed there was already a feeling that "we're someone" again because the community had its own paper. He pointed to a couple of stories that would never have been covered by the SVH: "Local Band Wins Battle of Bands" and an item about the Saukrates Conversation Group. They met once a month at Annie's Pizza, covering topics such as "What is good government?" and "What good is art?" The name of the group, Saukrates, was a nod both to the Socratic method and to Sauk Mountain, a prominent peak that serves as a backdrop to Concrete.

The geography here is central to the culture. As the two-lane North Cascades Highway wends eastward from Interstate 5, it climbs in elevation and moisture (Concrete gets an average of thirty-two inches of rain a year). Eventually, a forest of giant cedars and Douglas firs, dripping with moss and carpeted with ferns and blackberry bushes, flanks the road. The Skagit River is the highway's companion, beckoning a motorist to stop and gaze at its brilliant turquoise waters, their astonishing color provided by the palette of melting glaciers far upstream.

But like so many beautiful places, the area's isolation has a dark side for the people who live there. The highway becomes a dead-end road in the winter, when the Washington Pass closes because of snow and tourist traffic slows to a trickle. It's a tough place to make a living. Aside from seasonal tourism and a dwindling logging industry, jobs are scarce. Some locals work in the schools or local shops. But many are forced to drive long distances to find work—to Burlington and even Seattle, more than two hours away.

It was not always like this. The huge concrete plant that sits on the highway outside of Concrete is a monument to more profitable times. The confluence of the Baker and Skagit rivers is home to high-quality deposits of clay and limestone. The plant once made some of the best concrete in the world, at one point employing hundreds of people. The concrete was used to build the lower Baker River Dam in the 1920s, then the tallest dam in the world, and the Henry Thompson Bridge in Concrete, which—in its day—was the longest single-span cement bridge in the world.

And then there was the dust.

In the 1960s emissions from the plant averaged more than five hundred tons of dust per square mile each month. As one resident told the *Seattle Times*, "One nice thing: everybody drove the same color car."

The publisher-editor of the *Concrete Herald* at the time, Chuck Dwelley, led a crusade against the dust for more than forty years. "Wonder if a thousand years from now somebody will dig our city out of the cement dust," he wrote, "and wonder about what kind of people lived here?"

It didn't come to that, of course. The health of the people won out over the health of the economy in 1969, when new pollution laws forced the plant to close. The new North Cascades Highway included a bridge that bypassed the Henry Thompson Bridge, once the main route for crossing the Baker River. Concrete now sits a block off the main highway, which means travelers can easily drive right by without stopping.

There are now fewer than a thousand people living in Concrete. And the town is constantly looking for ways to reinvent itself, even holding a Dead Fly Festival. The one-time event, complete with a parade and a mock funeral, was a tongue-in-cheek reaction to a letter printed in the *Skagit Valley Herald* (yes, *that* paper again!) complaining about dead flies in the windows of Concrete restaurants. Other attempts at luring tourists to town have included a Bald Eagle Festival in February, when hundreds of the birds gather along the Skagit River. This event provides regular material for the police blotter:

> January 9 (2010): People caused a traffic hazard on State Route 20 near Marblemount because they were standing in the road, taking pictures of eagles. (That's right: IN the road). A deputy checked the area and also notified the Washington State Patrol and Darwin Award Officials.

One of the town's biggest claims to fame is the fact that author Tobias Wolff once lived there. His memoir about living in Concrete in the '50s was made into a movie starring Robert DeNiro and Leonardo DiCaprio called *This Boy's Life*. It is a grim tale, the kind that leaves you hoping that the boy, who is abused by his stepfather, will eventually manage to get out of town. Not exactly Chamber of Commerce material.

So what prompted young Jason Miller to choose Concrete, a place he hardly knew, for his journalistic venture? Was he looking to rescue a community and the First Amendment in one fell swoop?

Not really. He was looking for affordable real estate. The higher-minded stuff came later.

Miller had grown up in Lynden, Washington, a more affluent area and one where he could not afford to buy a home. He had been making a living as a freelance writer, specializing in home and garden articles, green building, and "new urbanism."

Armed with a loan from "the bank of mom and dad," he headed east and found Concrete. An avid backpacker and fisherman, he fell in love with the country. He bought a nice home near the river and dove into local politics, sitting on the planning commission and town council. And he saw a crying need for a town crier. The only "newspaper" in Concrete was the *Upriver Community News*, which was basically an advertising flyer with a few "articles." Local residents had no illusions that it was actual journalism. Merlene Buller, owner of the Sauk View Gallery, remembers submitting something she wanted the *Upriver Community News* to publish. She added at the bottom of her press release, "Please feel free to polish this." The editor printed her notice, exactly as written, complete with "feel free to polish this" at the bottom. She is thrilled that Miller has brought a new level of professionalism to the local news coverage.

"I was so sick of the quality of what we had," says Miller, "that I felt we deserved something better, a better reflection of us. It was atrocious!" As an example, he cites one article that was reprinted in the *Upriver Community News*, without any changes, for three years in a row. It described, in fractured English, an event in which local pilots staged a "fly-in."

Pilots, after what all of them seems to have accomplish, a superb landing, pull their planes off the runway-climb out onto the green grassy air field and relax-pulling out a lawn chair seating down to watch the next fight in or taking a stroll around exchanging stories, chatting with other pilots and the visiting crowd. Many spending the night for the next day's events—sleeping in camp bags under the wings of their plane, some in RV's other in local Hotels and some us the facilities provided by the Concrete Airport.

In other words, Jason Miller had no real competition.

Even so, he decided to purchase the *Upriver Community News* for four thousand dollars. "It was easier to buy the guy out than try to compete for the ad revenue," he says. He had no intention of using the name. Instead, he went to the museum, researched old papers in the area, and found the *Concrete Herald*. "Wow," he said to himself, "this was a good newspaper with solid reporting!" His plan was initially strategic. "My thinking," he recalls, "was that I would have instant 'street cred' by reviving the title." The font for the nameplate no longer existed, so he took a photo of that old woodcut title and made it into an image that appears on the top of each issue.

But what began as a logical business investment soon became an emotional investment. He was now part of this community, and as he prepared to revive the old *Concrete Herald*, he was bombarded with suggestions from local residents. He reminisced about that early pressure over breakfast, on my first day in town, at one of Concrete's three restaurants, just across the street from a small park whose centerpiece is an enormous wooden bear. According to the sign erected next to it, the bear, standing on its hind legs, was carved from a 1500-year-old Douglas fir donated by Georgia Pacific. It occurred to me that only in timber country would this be considered a good use for a 1500-year-old tree.

Miller had some cultural epiphanies of his own in his first year in Concrete. As he prepared to launch his paper, residents implored him to be a "good news" editor, not like those *Skagit*

Valley Herald folks. Most of their criticism was aimed at the way the svh had handled the story of a fourteen-year-old Concrete boy who had gone bear hunting with his brother on a popular trail on Sauk Mountain. The teenager, mistaking a woman hiker for a bear, had shot and killed her.

"The *Skagit Valley Herald* covered the snot out of that one," Miller tells me, "and people begged me not to be that kind of newspaper." What they meant by that, of course, was that they hoped he would have told that story in a light favorable to the local boy, framing it as a tragic accident rather than as a reckless disregard for human life. The cultural fault lines pitted the old-timers' love of hunting against the newcomers' love of hiking.

Miller came up with a simple response to those pressures. "I told them, 'I'm not creating a newsletter, but a newspaper.'" The boy ended up getting off easy, he says, sentenced to thirty days in juvenile hall plus community service and no fine. Even so, many residents were outraged (as were the dead woman's friends and relatives, for different reasons), and this was all he heard about leading up to the launch of the *Concrete Herald*.

The cultural pressures paled, however, in comparison to the financial pressures. He finally managed to raise enough money in donations and advertising revenue to invest in Mac equipment for his home, which serves as his one-man newsroom. He launched the paper, which started as a monthly with mail subscriptions costing twenty-four dollars per year, in the spring of 2009. He also has a free Web site where he posts a small sampling of articles from each issue. "I don't believe in giving away all the paper's content for free," he says. And he probably doesn't have to. While we were lining up for the parade, a man approached him and said that he had moved to North Carolina but was in town for a reunion of the Concrete High class of

1959. He signed up for a subscription immediately, right there on the street. Where else, he asked, can I learn about what my old friends are doing back home?

Miller is also seeing more ad revenue with each issue. The local merchants are thrilled to appeal to customers through a newspaper that locals actually want to read. "The paper is awesome," says Sherrill Coville, owner of Matty's On Main gift shop. "This is MY paper," she claims proudly, adding that she never did read—or advertise in—the *Skagit Valley Herald*.

Miller never planned to get rich at this, of course. He just wants to make a decent living in a town he has come to love. And there is another downside. "My social life is in the toilet," he says with a rueful grin, echoing a common complaint of small-town editors who take on this 24-7 job without the support of an understanding soul mate.

And so, for now, his passion is reserved for the paper. Good thing, since it is a relentless job for one person. The *Concrete Herald* is printed in Everett at the *Daily Herald* offices. "They wanted $120 to deliver it to me in Concrete," says Miller, "so I tried to save $70 by meeting their delivery truck at the intersection of I-5 and Highway 20. But the meet time was 1:30 a.m. and I'm not 20 anymore." So now he drives all the way to Everett the night before and picks up the papers himself. "That way," he says with a grin, "on the way home, I can stuff all the newspaper boxes along the highway!"

He brings that same optimism and "can-do" spirit to the articles in the paper. He loves positive news, he says, and so the *Herald* has a whole section called "SMILE," which includes "Dwelley-isms," quotes he has gleaned from the writings of one of the first editors, Chuck Dwelley. Some examples:

The Clallam County treasurer who managed to steal $38,000

in cash during his term in office should reveal to the various civic organizations how he managed to get that much money away from the commissioners without a petition.

The yardstick for advertising is simple: if you can afford a sign on your door, you can afford to advertise. If you can afford a showroom or display window, you should advertise. If you can afford neither, man, you'd *better* advertise!

All it takes is a careful perusal of the daily papers to make one realize that Concrete is a mighty fine place in which to live.

If you want to find out how many friends you have, seek an office in a small town election.

Apparently, nostalgia sells. Another feature, entitled "Way Back When," reprints old articles from the original *Herald*. A local resident I spoke with called it his favorite section. One story in particular reminded him of his days in grade school. "The father of a girl in our class fell off the dam and was killed," he told me. "They found his body in Lake Shannon, but it took awhile. Until then, the family couldn't get the insurance and had no means of support." Reading the old article about that body being found, he said, "brought it all back like it was yesterday."

Meanwhile, the events of today keep on coming, and Miller has found a way to spread the burden. He now uses volunteers from the various towns he covers along Highway 20 to contribute local articles. These pieces aren't always "objective," but they give new meaning to the term "citizen journalism." Miller has enlisted area residents to file not-so-dispassionate dispatches about their school teams and games, for example.

Local boosterism aside, Miller is committed to a fair parsing of the facts. He got to test that commitment early on when he received a tip that a local food bank operated by two religious groups had been ransacked.

"I called the pastor of the Hamilton First Baptist Church, which, along with the Christian Ministry Network, runs the food bank in Hamilton," says Miller, "but I got a cold shoulder. 'Don't do this story,' he told me, 'it will just divide the community.'" Miller told the pastor, "'When a food bank gets ransacked and stripped of all its goods in a small town, that belongs in a small-town newspaper. Asking me not to cover it would be like ME marching into your church and asking YOU not to mention Matthew, Mark, Luke and John that week.'" The young editor smiles, remembering. "He understood that!"

It turns out that the "ransacking" (more of a clearance operation, actually) had been carried out by folks from the other religious group—the Christian Ministry Network. They accused the Baptists of violating federal funding rules by "proselytizing to people waiting in line for food" and so decided to take the goods somewhere else for distribution to the poor.

Miller wrote about all of it. The community survived.

This is not to say, however, that he will never confront the "too close for comfort" problem experienced by small-town editors, especially since he still holds his seat on the town council. Anne Bussiere, who served as editor back in 1991, says, "I told him he should give up his town council seat. He can't do both." When I told her that Jason's plan was to hire a reporter to cover any controversial story involving the council, she laughed. "Well, I'm not going to be that reporter," she stated, remembering earlier days when she held that job for the *Herald*, covering lengthy council meetings and "debates about every little sewer line" for ten dollars an article.

Miller's two roles may yet collide. As he gave me a quick tour of Concrete, he pointed out a neighborhood where yards were filled with rusting piles of junk, including old cars. "This is one of the first things I'm going to tackle," he said. "These are in violation of existing laws."

"Sounds like a good story," I replied.

"Oh, no," came the response. "I meant I want to tackle it as part of my town council work." And then, seeing my expression, he added, "I'll have to assign someone else to write that story."

Al Cross, director of the Institute for Rural Journalism and Community Issues at the University of Kentucky, says, "I think editors should stay at arms' length from the politics of the town they cover," but he adds, "I don't like to preach from the ivory tower of the university campus because that's the quickest way to get people to stop listening." The reality, he acknowledges, is that in some towns "there is such a lack of civic leadership, that the editors just step in and say, 'someone has to do this.' It can be beneficial for the town in the short term, but it's almost always inadvisable."

When I last checked, Jason Miller was still trying to straddle the roles of the watchdog and the watched without biting himself in the editorial ass. So far, not a single reader of the *Concrete Herald* has complained about the fairness of the coverage. Perhaps they are simply too grateful—grateful that someone cared enough to dust off a beloved old relic and give it and their community new life.

Speaking of new life, M. E. Sprengelmeyer not only reinvented a local paper, he reinvented himself in the process. Sprengelmeyer (who stopped going by Michael E. Sprengelmeyer because his full name wouldn't fit in a byline) used to be the Washington correspondent for the *Rocky Mountain News*. He covered the 9/11 attack on the Pentagon and the presidential campaign of Barack

Obama, and he reported from the battlefields of Afghanistan and Iraq. He was the *Rocky*'s watchdog-at-large. "Now," he says (happily), "my watchdog role is watching who gets married."

In 2009, shortly after the E. W. Scripps Company announced it was closing the *Rocky Mountain News* just shy of its 150th birthday, Sprengelmeyer made an unusual career move. He coughed up a good portion of his life savings and purchased the sixth-smallest weekly in his home state of New Mexico, the *Guadalupe County Communicator*, in the small town of Santa Rosa. He is now its owner, publisher, editor, chief writer, and occasional ad salesman. He also delivers the paper.

Like Jason Miller's efforts to start a small-town paper, Sprengelmeyer's decision to take over a small-town paper was deemed a newsworthy event in itself. The *New York Times* sent a reporter to Santa Rosa to check out this radical career move. "Of the thousands of paths taken by journalists who have been cast off by shrinking metropolitan newspapers," wrote *Times* reporter Richard Perez-Pena, "Mr. Sprengelmeyer's is one of the more unusual, and one of the more hopeful. While bringing some big-city professionalism to a distinctly small-time operation, he says he is making enough money to support himself, and he has been able to assign some freelance work to a few underemployed former colleagues."

"It's the Tom Sawyer business plan," Sprengelmeyer told the *Times*. "I'm trying to convince all my friends how much fun it would be to help me." One of those former colleagues willing to lend a hand is Mark Holm, a photographer and former photo editor of the now-defunct *Rocky*. The very first issue of the *Communicator* (August 6, 2009) under Sprengelmeyer's editorial control featured a stunning front-page shot of a cowboy and his girlfriend sitting atop a pickup truck at the Guadalupe County Fair Ranch Rodeo. They are silhouetted against a dramatic New Mexico sunset, leaning in for a kiss.

Sprengelmeyer's accompanying article about the fair matches the professional quality of the photo. But it also demonstrates that he "gets it" when it comes to the values and traditions of rural America.

Devyn Sisneros finally got his reward last weekend for all the 5 a.m. wake-up calls and the chores that came with them.

On a hot, summer morning at a sun-baked Santa Rosa fairgrounds, the 16-year-old took home a grand champion award at the Guadalupe County Fair for "Gus," a calm, quiet, 189-pound hog he had raised at his family's ranch in Colonias.

To many, the annual fair is about non-stop family entertainment, like the popular Ranch Rodeo, live musical concerts, summer foods and more. But it's all designed to celebrate rural values and reward hard work at a time when agriculture is under constant pressure from economic conditions and other factors, like the lure of careers in the cities.

This town of 2,600 people sat up and took notice. Issue after issue has featured this sort of professional coverage of local events and people, with stunning photos to match. It certainly caught the attention of the editor of the other paper in town, the *Santa Rosa News*. Roberto Martin Marquez even took time to pay Sprengelmeyer a compliment. "M. E. is making me a better newspaper man," he wrote in his paper.

Sprengelmeyer says he hopes to inspire other laid-off, big-city reporters to do what he is doing. "I think it's going to be a renaissance for small-town journalism," he told me. His career move was not an impulsive thing. As he traveled the country covering the Obama campaign in the year before the *Rocky* closed, he "kicked the tires," in his words, "at some quaint, little newspapers that were for sale all around the country." In the end, he decided to return to his home state (he grew up in Albuquerque). The *Guadalupe County Communicator* was everything he was looking for: the tiny town of Santa Rosa (population 2,600) is located on historic Route 66, a two-hour drive east of Albuquerque, where Highway 40 crosses the Pecos River. The town boasts of good fishing and camping sites (its slogan is "The City of Natural Lakes") and a famous desert scuba-diving site, a ninety-foot-deep cenote called "The Blue Hole." The geography and local market economy, which attracts a number of tourists, convinced him that Santa Rosa could support the kind of paper he wanted to produce.

"Small-town newspapers," Sprengelmeyer wrote in the blog savethenews.org, "use a business model that is like a miniature version of where the big-city newspapers are heading. They are forced to stay within their means. They have tiny staffs—only what the day-to-day cash flow can sustain. They aren't afraid of reader-generated content. They outsource many functions, such as printing and distribution. And, often by accident, they keep their communities addicted to the print product because they don't give away a whole lot of material for free on the internet."

He does have plans for a Web site, but he will design it around news that would interest "tourists, fisherfolks, scuba divers, Billy the Kid chasers, and Route 66 fans" who would not be interested in "school board stuff, city hall stuff, school sports stuff." The goal, Sprengelmeyer tells me, "is to have our local residents visit the site one time, roll their eyes, and go away hungry for the local news that's only provided in the printed product."

"In small towns like Santa Rosa," he believes, "the future of print is print."

Even so, the challenge of operating the paper, including the workload, has humbled him. In addition to one fulltime writer and an ad designer, he has the photographer Holm and an editorial cartoonist from the *Rocky* who regularly contribute their talents. "I wasn't planning to write," he tells me, "but my standards are too high." About half the bylines in the eighteen or so pages of the *Communicator*, in fact, are his, making for an exhausting week. "I slept three hours a night for three nights in a row before my first edition," he says, "and that hasn't changed much." And he personally makes the three-hour-roundtrip drive to Clovis, where the paper is printed each week, to pick up the press run, making deliveries on his return, just as Jason Miller does in Concrete. And, like Jason, he is a bachelor. Life would be easier, he concedes, if he were part of a husband-and-wife team like the previous owners.

One of those owners, Jesus Roybal, was also the town administrator, giving the *Communicator* a definite political slant. The other weekly, the *Santa Rosa News*, was aligned with Roybal's rivals in city hall and its copy reflected that bias. That gave Sprengelmeyer a distinct professional advantage as the wordslinger from out of town. "People are hugging me for bringing a fair eye" to covering the town's political scene, he says.

Not that the political showdowns are anything like those Sprengelmeyer used to cover on Capitol Hill. In Santa Rosa, the biggest controversy he has covered involved plans for a giant water slide that the town council had purchased to create an amusement park. "The original goal of turning it into a tourism magnet here has never gotten off the ground," he wrote in October 2009. "And so the ground is where the equipment remains, spread across an area the size of a football field as a sort of monument to civic dreams unfulfilled."

But covering "smaller" stories, he notes, has made him a

better journalist. "It's real humbling for me," he says. "I'm no longer writing one long story, and calling it a day." Even as he is selling ads, planning the layout, or writing an article, he has to be ready to drop everything and run to a breaking story. His coverage of two recent fires, for example, included not only dramatic photos of the homes ablaze but also compassionate articles about the families who had lost everything, prompting an outpouring of charity from the townspeople. The loss of a "manufactured" home, with its sparse furnishings, can be overwhelming in a town where the per capita income is less than half the national average. As Sprengelmeyer wrote on savethenews.org, "A community newspaper has a physical presence. It's not faceless. It is accountable to the people who live next door. It connects one neighbor to the next."

Now that he is one of those neighbors, he has no regrets (except, perhaps, over a lack of sleep and a social life) about moving to this small town on a prairie of mesquite and juniper. In his first Thanksgiving edition, under the headline "On top of everything, I'm thankful for news," he wrote:

> I've lived in many other places, and in a lot of those places I could go many months, or even years, waiting to meet more than a handful of my neighbors. Here, if I tried to list all the people who've stopped by to introduce themselves, then this page would look like one of those small-type legal ads in the back of the paper.

> Most of all, though, this holiday season I am thankful to be in a place where newspapers aren't just read, they're valued.

> In this age where papers all across the country are struggling or dying, Guadalupe County is proving the naysayers wrong.

Hopefully, we're showing how newspapers can survive and thrive—and that's with ever-improving content and great community participation.

Each day, I'm astounded by how many people walk into the newsroom to shoot the breeze, offer story tips, articles, photographs, encouragement, guidance or ideas for things we could be doing better.

It makes me glad I put my desk right up front near the door.

CHAPTER TWO

Crusaders

One night in 1961, in the small town of Canadian, Texas, nine-year-old Laurie Ezzell awoke to the sound of a rock crashing through her bedroom window. It left a hole in the screen and shattered the glass. She was startled but not surprised. "Dad's written another editorial," she thought.

Her father, Ben Ezzell, had purchased the *Canadian Record* in this Panhandle town in 1948 and promptly established a reputation as a fiercely independent, stubborn maverick, a reputation that followed him all the way to the obituary page. ("Cussed and Discussed" was the headline on his 1993 obit in the *Amarillo Globe*.) The rock hurled through his daughter's window was typical of readers' reactions to his more controversial stands. On that particular occasion, the article was an exposé of a little-known group called the John Birch Society. Ezzell warned his readers not to join "if you place any value on your own freedom." The story was reprinted around the country, and the *Record* got more than its usual share of angry letters.

By the late '60s, Ezzell had moved on to other issues: the Vietnam War, for one. "I am ashamed of what my country is doing in this war, in my name and in the name of all of us," he wrote in one of his weekly columns in 1968. One local businessman was so angry he said he would quit advertising in the *Canadian Record* and tried to organize a boycott by the merchants in town. Ironically, he only had one good way to get the word out.

Ben Ezzell sold him a half-page ad.

The boycott failed. And Ezzell kept writing. Following another editorial against the war in 1971, someone fired a pellet gun through a door and window at the newspaper's office. Ezzell's response: "Someone was expressing an editorial opinion," adding, "It is a great American privilege." But over the years, Ezzell's paper took on issues that did lose him advertisers and, now and then, even friends. In the words of another journalist, Jim Reynolds of the *Tulia Herald*, "I don't suppose there's a fence in captivity that Ben Ezzell ever straddled." And that often made it very tough on his family.

The backlash from their father's outspoken editorial policy in this small town of 2,300 was hard on all six Ezzell children but especially on the youngest, who were in high school during the turbulent sixties. But wimping out was not an option. Laurie, the youngest daughter and the one who would grow up to take her father's place, says that "toughness is the genetic curse of the family." Genetic, perhaps, but also forged clearly in her father's weekly habit of practicing the First Amendment with such gusto. She and her siblings grew up being very aware of political issues, and both parents encouraged them to express their opinions. At the same time, she says, they had to answer for their dad's liberal political views.

"It was hard to be a teenager wanting to blend in," Laurie recalls. She was always singled out after her father had written something controversial, like this editorial on the death of Martin Luther King Jr.:

It is easy to deal in fine words and platitudes in our all white-community where we are scarcely touched, as yet, by the problems of racial strife. [But] we can try to put an end to the attitude which we have too much of still: that the Negro is somehow an inferior, an object of scorn, or of derision. We can put an end to the sort of remarks we overheard on Friday from a local woman: "well, they call him a doctor, but I don't know what he's a doctor of!" Dr. King, whose education was excellent and whose degrees were earned, would not have bothered to feel personally insulted by that sort of remark. But he would, we feel sure, have been saddened and outraged by the attitude it reveals toward the people of his race.

The subsequent taunts aimed at Laurie—"nigger-lover" was typical—made her feel even more alienated, she says. "One kid yelled, 'How are things in Moscow today, Laurie?'"

And teenage pranksters continued to target the Ezzell home with garden-variety projectiles: tomatoes and watermelons. "We never knew who had done it," says Laurie, "and that was the most difficult thing for us kids, not knowing exactly who, at any given moment, hated us the most."

Nor could she look to the teachers for help. After all, this was a high school whose dress code read, in part: "Long hair has come to classify an unhealthy, irresponsible, subversive un-American reactionary attitude and personality." In fact, Laurie almost failed her civics class, required for graduation, after she had a confrontation with the teacher over a chart hung on the wall. "She had marked up parts of the Bill of Rights she thought were too liberal," remembers Laurie. The teacher claimed that these "liberal" sections were allowing communism to spread in the United States. But Laurie, the editor of her high school paper, knew something about the power of exposure. "I took a photo of it and the next day it was gone."

It became an early lesson in what can happen to whistleblowers: the teacher would later falsely accuse Laurie of cheating on a test. Suddenly, she was in danger of flunking. "She made me read J. Edgar Hoover's book and write an essay on it so I could graduate." Even though she is telling this story some forty years later, the sense of injustice still smarts. Righting wrongs is something the Ezzells take seriously.

Now, if all you knew about Canadian, Texas, came from these few anecdotes, you might wonder why anyone with a scintilla of sense would stay there more than a day. But the Ezzells love this community. Laurie's affection for it—especially given those tough teenage years in the sixties—is surprisingly passionate.

Even for this visitor, the outward charms of Canadian, at least, were almost immediately apparent, especially after the drive from Amarillo: mile after mile of straight-ahead, no-relief blandness, broken only by the occasional dying town, abandoned homestead, or crippled windmill; endless freight trains with their mournful whistles; stray tufts of cotton impaled on barbed-wire fences; and always, endlessly, a coma-inducing flatness. As one local told me, "In Amarillo, you can see your dog run away for three days."

And then, just as I was wondering, "Why on earth would anyone live here?" the topography transformed, the road dipped and curved, and I found myself driving under stately cottonwoods, along the Canadian River, as the road wended its way, at long last, into the town of Canadian.

My first impression was that I had been inserted into a scene from the film *Back to the Future*. The old art deco movie theater, "The Palace," has been restored to its original splendor, with light bulbs around the marquee. Next door, also restored to its 1910 marble-countered, confectionary magnificence, is the City Drug Soda Fountain. Just up the street is the only building in the United States ever built and owned by a local chapter of the Women's Christian Temperance Union (WCTU). The WCTU hosts the annual Christmas bazaar and turkey dinner, which just celebrated a hundredth anniversary that I had the good fortune to attend. Apparently, over the years, the good ladies have made up in food what they once surrendered in drink. There is clearly no "temperance" in this meal: heaps of turkey with all the fixings; pies of every description; and, of course, that staple of middle America, ambrosia salad (key ingredient: miniature marshmallows). The servers, cheery women dressed in aprons appliquéd with appropriate seasonal icons, reminded me immediately of my grandmothers cooking up a "mess" of artery-clogging treats in my parents' hometown of Milton-Freewater, Oregon.

Let's face it, some charms cannot be explained rationally.

Across the street from the movie theatre is the office of the *Canadian Record*. On the day of my visit, which was the day the paper comes out, there was a sign in the window that read, "NEWSPAPER NOT HERE YET." Actually, it *was* there, but the meager staff was still in a back room inserting the advertising circulars in all the copies. A lot of things about newspapering have changed—digital has replaced linotype, for example—but human beings still have to stuff the circulars. And those circulars represent revenue. And so they patiently stand and stuff, week after week.

The reason for the sign, explains Laurie, is crowd control. On Thursday morning, when the papers are delivered from the printer in nearby Liberal, Kansas, the residents of Canadian start showing up early to get their copies. Parking becomes a problem. The residents here are hungry for local news, the kind that no other outlet can provide. One loyal reader, says Laurie, was "old Doc Echols [now deceased], who would drive in from the country and sit on the bench in front of the grocery store every week to wait for the paper to be delivered. No one told him that I was giving the staff Christmas week off and we heard that he sat there all day that week. I apologized to him when I heard about it."

Laurie's father believed that the paper was so vital to the community that he never took a week off, not for a family vacation, not even for Christmas. Nan Ezzell, Laurie's mother, started helping out at the paper in the early years because her husband had hired some people "who couldn't spell beans," she tells me. Besides, Nan adds, if she had not joined in, she would have been a "linotype widow" and resented all the time he spent at the office. At ninety years old, she prides herself on being a journalist and a top-notch proofreader. She still serves as coeditor with Laurie (now Laurie Ezzell Brown), and until recently, still continued to write her weekly column, "Petticoat Patter," a look at the social doings around town.

"Mom provided a critical balance to dad. She was a moderating voice, a huge booster of the town," says Laurie. In one column on a regional drama contest, Nan praised the competing group of high school girls in this way: "That the Canadian play did not win was probably due more to personal preferences of the judges than to any lack of excellence of performance on the part of the cast."

That's Texas-polite for "we got screwed."

Sometimes Nan would use this petticoat patois to sneak in a bit of feminist commentary. "For some time," Nan wrote in 1968, "it has seemed to me, and to other women with whom I have talked, that a woman's ideas, thoughts, and influence on the Canadian School Board would very possibly be beneficial to all concerned. A woman looks at some things with a different viewpoint from that of men and it is a viewpoint which has been missing from our school board."

This fairly revolutionary idea (for Canadian, anyway) came at the bottom of the column, after items about New Eyeglasses for the Needy and a recital by the Pampa Community Concert Association. In other words, Nan could bury a lead with the best of them. And no one lobbed rocks at the house.

Nan has no plans to retire and is thrilled that the paper is still in the hands of her family. "If there were no paper," she says, "no one would know about community and school events and the politicians would know that no one was watching."

And if those politicians thought someone was looking over their shoulders when Ben Ezzell was editor, they had a truly rude awakening when his daughter took over after his death in 1993. "My Dad had no staff," remembers Laurie. "It was just him and mom and me. And he worked his tail off." Even so, she says, he didn't have time to attend meetings. He would talk to elected officials after the meeting was over and take their word for what had happened. "That was one area where I didn't like how he handled it."

And so Laurie, who now has five salaried employees, started showing up at each and every meeting of the town council and the county commissioners and the school board.

The school superintendent's initial reaction: "What are you doing here? Your DADDY never did that!"

And then the superintendent did his best to discourage her.

The school board met in a small room, says Laurie, with double doors. They reluctantly opened those doors when she complained and placed a chair in the doorway. "But they had high-backed chairs and I still couldn't hear them," she says. So one of her first stories about the school board pointed out that public meetings should make room for the public.

The board moved to a larger room.

But it was a short-lived victory, because the board members would regularly vote to go into "executive session," even though they could give her no legal justification.

She wrote about that, too.

But they weren't done. "They would start their meetings at seven and go to three in the morning, hoping they could outlast me," says Laurie.

They didn't.

"Finally, the superintendent's wife came into the [*Canadian Record*] office and yelled, 'Your Daddy wouldn't have done it this way!'" Laurie tells me, reveling in the memory. "And I said, 'No, but he would have defended my right to do it this way.'"

But doing it her way wasn't easy, especially when she tried to cover a meeting of the county hospital administrators. Her brother Robert happened to be the hospital's chief administrator. "He would call executive sessions that were not properly posted," says Laurie. She showed him the law on the subject, but "he didn't react well to that."

"I didn't write about it at first," she says, because her brother "is well-thought-of in this town, almost like a saint." But then she decided, in the interest of fairness, that she had to report this breach the same way she had reported others. Her brother did not speak to her for months after the article appeared. Her mother was none too pleased, either, along with some friends who scolded, "Shame on you for picking on your brother!"

Still, no one would ever be able to accuse Laurie of playing favorites. "I couldn't let it pass," says Laurie. "It's like when people call and ask you to keep their names out of the police blotter. And I say, 'Would you ever believe the blotter again?' There has to be consistency or you lose your credibility. Bottom line, that's all we've got." She and her brother are once again on good speaking terms. And executive sessions are always properly posted.

Laurie was not afraid to take on powerful interests outside the family, either, even when it involved going after those with the means to retaliate. Richard Roach, for one. In the late '90s, he was a candidate for the district attorney's office. He came from a well-respected Baptist family in the area and sang in the church choir. But Laurie had heard rumors that Roach had a bad cocaine habit and was even smuggling drugs.

"I spent hours on the phone every night with people who knew him," says Laurie. "But I didn't have time for a full time investigation and I didn't have enough corroboration to print any of this. So I just decided to talk to him and get his response," adding, "I'm not trained in journalism, so it's all I knew to do."

At first, Roach didn't want to talk. "He said, 'They told me about you. They told me you're a feminazi and a liberal and you hate men.' And I said, 'Two out of three ain't bad.'" It was only after he read her interview in the paper with his opponent, a Democrat, that he decided to get some equal time. Much to her surprise, he admitted that he had a drug problem, although he claimed it was behind him.

Roach lost that election (to a Democrat!) and blamed the paper. So he sued for libel. "We had never been sued for libel, and it cost us," Laurie recalls. "Especially since he acted as his own attorney and it cost him nothing" to bleed the paper.

He finally dropped the lawsuit, she says, but it cost the paper thousands of dollars and valuable time. Meanwhile, Roach ran again for district attorney and won. "Now we had a very powerful enemy," says Laurie. "He was a very volatile man and it was a very scary time. A lot of people were angry with me for saying all those things about him."

And so you might think the Ezzells would have wallowed in a bit of well-deserved schadenfreude when District Attorney Richard Roach was finally charged with drug and weapons possession. He pleaded guilty. "Vindication is pretty sweet," says Laurie, "and a lot of those people who said I was a terrible person for saying those things about Rich Roach had trouble looking me in the eye. Even so," she adds, "his kids had to listen to all this in court. I had compassion for his family. There was no glory in it."

This ability to temper her sense of justice with fairness and compassion is what makes Laurie Ezzell Brown so highly respected, despite the fact that she is a liberal in a conservative Texas community with powerful oil and gas interests. Perhaps no story illustrates her unique position as clearly as the homicide trial Laurie describes as one of "the hardest stories she has had to do."

A two-year-old boy, Brendan Brown, had been beaten to death, allegedly by the live-in boyfriend of Brendan's single mother, seventeen-year-old Caryn Brown. Laurie says the sordid details and graphic postmortem images displayed during the trial were tough to witness and even harder to report.

"They were brutal, unbearably sad images of a child so bruised and battered that his blood seemed to have gathered just below the surface of his skin, pooling and darkening there," wrote Laurie in one of her columns. "Angry red burn marks, perfect round O's in the shape of a tiny mouth—a mouth that is frozen in terror and disbelief—pocked his face and arms, speaking another language, conveying their own horrifying story."

Laurie drove to Amarillo to report on the trial, coverage that got her targeted by angry friends and relatives of the mother and boyfriend. "I was taunted as I walked out of the courtroom. They had no conscience, no sense of guilt. It was creepy, with a pervasive air of threat." When the windows of her car were shot out, says Laurie, she knew it was not random vandalism.

After the mother, Caryn Brown, a hardcore drug user, refused to testify against the boyfriend, the jurors voted "not guilty." But most people in Canadian believed otherwise, including Laurie. Even so, she printed a long "Letter to the Editor" that Caryn Brown hand delivered to the *Record*'s office. In the letter, the teenage mother continued to deny any involvement in her son's brutal death and instead railed at the town for making her life "a hell on earth."

Laurie responded in her column, saying, "So it is Canadian that is guilty, now? Guilty of harsh judgment without knowing the facts? No, Caryn, we know too much." Once again, time would deliver justice. The boyfriend and his mother were later arrested for witness tampering, and Caryn Brown went to prison for reckless endangerment of a child.

And once again, Laurie was not interested in wallowing in a moment of "I told you so." When Caryn Brown was released from prison after three years, she started classes at Amarillo College to get a degree as a substance abuse counselor. As much as Laurie had railed against the abuse and neglect that led to the death of two-year-old Brendan, she printed an interview with Brown in which the former meth addict took responsibility for her past actions and talked about her newfound faith. Now, says Laurie, Caryn Brown is helping others in the community overcome their drug addiction.

Unlike crime stories in the mainstream media, which end with the verdict, stories in small-town weeklies have time to evolve. And while the mainstream media may have to worry about libel suits, they do not have to worry about living next door to the folks they cover. "I take some comfort," says Laurie, "that I have to live with the consequences of my stories. I have to look this person in the eye. I have to know I have written the right thing."

Over the years, "the right thing" has resulted in real changes. In 1995 Laurie started reporting about plans by large-scale corporate hog farming operations to come to Hemphill County. "They were moving into every county in the Panhandle," she says. Laurie had heard rumors about deals between state lawmakers and the hog farming industry—"pork barrel politics" in the most literal sense—but she could not prove them. She only knew that the Panhandle had a reputation as a political dumping ground—a place, she says, "for pigs, plutonium pits, and prisons."

Laurie and her reporters decided to take the offensive. Their research showed that while hog farms may have brought some Panhandle landowners a nice payoff and the counties some added revenue, they left behind toxic waste that polluted one of the region's most precious commodities: the groundwater supply. Her articles and editorials raised enough alarms that the Hemphill County commissioners were finally persuaded. They passed a resolution saying they would not offer hog farm operations any tax incentives for locating in the county.

The pork went elsewhere.

"There's no job like this," says Laurie. "You can really stop bad things from happening. And it's never dull."

And she means never. Her desk sits at the front of the

newspaper office, which lies in the middle of Main Street. Stories walk through the door all day long. So do irate readers. Her late father, Ben Ezzell, used to tell the story of a man who strode in one day and announced, "I've just driven two thousand miles to whip your ass!" The man, who mistakenly believed that Ezzell had written something disrespectful about his parents (allegedly regarding dead dogs found in their swimming pool), was packing 250 pounds worth of muscle and "a pair of ears that showed evidence of some not-overly-successful experience in the boxing ring." Ezzell, in contrast, was all of 130 pounds and sported the musculature of someone who sat in front of a typewriter most of the day. And he was alone in the office.

His response to this threat to whip his skinny ass? According to his recollection in his biography, "I laughed and said, 'It doesn't look like it was hardly worth the trip, does it?'" And with that, he broke the tension and got the man to explain what his gripe was all about. When Ezzell was able to reassure him that he had never written an article about dead dogs in a swimming pool (it was a complicated rumor), the man "glared for a few minutes, turned and slammed through the door, then, sticking his head back inside, got in the last word: "You'd better not write anything about them dogs!'"

It would not be the last time someone threatened to whip his ass, or the editorial equivalent, and Laurie would inherit her father's gift for defusing such situations. She also inherited the gift for listening patiently to drop-ins who were sure they were on to a big story, invariably one in which they were the victims. While I was visiting, a couple of local teachers came in with some documents purportedly showing that the Canadian superintendent of schools was making much more, and the teachers much less, than the state average. They asked Laurie if she would "look into it"—meaning, of course, that they wanted her to do the heavy lifting on their behalf. She said she would.

Laurie found that the numbers were not so cut and dried, and she decided not to write an article about such a fuzzy disparity. But she encouraged the teachers to write letters to the editor. They did, and the result was a new salary schedule passed by the school board, complete with a pay raise.

And they talk about "citizen journalism" as though it's something new.

Laurie's staff of five shares her watchdog intensity. They don't make much money, and there is not enough for company health insurance, but they are intensely loyal and believe in the paper's "Statement of Policy," first espoused by Ben Ezzell. It reads, in part: "We believe in the freedom of the press. We are grateful for it. We will defend it to the limit of our ability. We believe, too, that in return for that freedom, we owe an obligation of service to our community. . . . We believe that an informed public is our best guarantee of freedom." Of course, a sense of purpose is great, but it doesn't pay the bills. One way Laurie keeps such a loyal staff is by pouring profits back into the paper; "every time we do better, I bump up salaries and give bonuses."

Some issues sell better than others, and Laurie counts on special editions for revenue. When the high school in Canadian won the state football championship in its division, for example, the paper was over thirty pages long and jam-packed with ads. She counts on those good weeks to offset the inevitable backlash when she speaks out on a controversial issue.

She did exactly that during the presidential primary campaign in her column "Field Notes." She wrote about a visit to her newspaper office by "two of my elders and fellow Democrats." They came to talk about politics in general and their dislike of Barack Obama in particular.

Believing, I suppose, that I am a sympathizer, both men affirm their staunch opposition to presidential candidate Barack Obama—which is fine—in terms that raise haunting images of the Deep South, white sheets and burning crosses—which is not.

I feel shame and rage, but I also feel the stirrings of resolve as my now-unwelcome guests depart.

Laurie did not report exactly what they said, which included the phrase "you know how those niggers are." She was so upset by their casual racism, so angry that these were fellow members of the Democratic Party (a rare breed in Canadian), that she told them, "PLEASE LEAVE." They threw down their newspapers and walked out.

And Laurie sat down at her computer:

Their vitriol and animosity infuse this office with a stink I had thought, hoped, and prayed—though never quite dared to believe—long gone from my hometown. My stomach roils in remembrance of similar words spoken to me as a child.

Quite coincidentally . . . a bound file of the *Record* from the 1930s sits at the corner of my desk. I had dug it out of the stacks and dusted it off days before to fill in some sizeable gaps in my knowledge of Canadian's past.

I know, by now, what I will find buried in those yellowed pages: the report of a baseball game between a local club and a traveling team. The headline that crowns that story, "Canadian Loses to Colored Team," is a sickening reminder of a past we can't escape. The story is a remarkable piece of date-stamped journalism—bad journalism, mind you, littered with grotesque allusions to the visiting team's skin color and their general inferiority as human beings. . . .

The past has visited me in two old men, their voices cracked with age, their faces creased with time and hints of sorrow, their fear and hatred so long held, so resistant to thought, that it has calcified. . . .

Perhaps the Democratic Party will rise again in this country . . . but if it rises, it will not be on the shoulders of men like these, who still hate and fear and long for a time when the white man's supremacy was unchallenged. It will be on my shoulders and on yours, and on the shoulders of men like Barack Obama, who dare to dream again of a better America, an America that has found its way.

I ask Laurie about the backlash. She had to have known, I say, that writing those words would mean cutting off her connections to those fellow Democrats.

She expected the same thing. So she was dumbfounded when they had both come back into the office, weeks later, as though nothing had happened. "I was stunned, just stunned."

One of the men asked if she would help organize a Democratic caucus. He never mentioned their previous dust-up or her angry column.

"I can't figure it out," she says, "but I decided I'm not going to dwell on it."

She's been much too busy to dwell on it. Too many stories to cover, never enough time. Not even enough time, apparently, for the family to repair that screen on her childhood bedroom window. The hole carved out by that late-night "editorial opinion," says Laurie, is still there.

A few years ago, the Ezzell family was honored with the Gish Award for courage and tenacity in rural journalism. The award, created by the Institute for Rural Journalism and Community

Issues (IRJCI), is named for Tom and Pat Gish, the husband-and-wife team who truly set the standard for small-town editorial bravery with their half-century stewardship of the *Mountain Eagle* in Whitesburg, Kentucky.

No chapter about crusaders in journalism—rural or otherwise—would be complete without them.

"Mr. Gish and his wife, Pat," wrote the *New York Times*, "overcame floods, threats, arson, and attempted suppression to deliver" the news, week after week, without fail. "TomAndPat," says longtime friend and contributing editor Tom Bethell, "was always one word. Pat made it all possible—she did 85 percent of the work of getting the paper out, while Tom fulminated at his typewriter. They didn't start out to be crusaders. It was thrust upon them. And they rose to the occasion."

Tom Gish died in 2008 at the age of eighty-two. Pat Gish now suffers from Alzheimer's and is no longer able to work at the paper. Their son, Ben, has taken over as editor.

"We always had a family joke," Ben tells me in his thick Appalachian twang, "that you could get an issue of the *Mountain Eagle* from the sixties or seventies, just change the names, and the stories would be the same." Sometimes, he adds, we would "worry that nothing has changed. But once my dad retired and was able to reflect, he did think he had made a difference."

A big difference, by most accounts. National Public Radio's Howard Berkes points out that "some people say Lyndon Johnson's War on Poverty began with stories in the *Mountain Eagle*."

But let's back up a bit, to the 1950s. Tom returned to his hometown of Whitesburg in the heart of Kentucky coal country after a stint as a reporter with United Press International. "Tom was very proud of being from eastern Kentucky," says Bethell. "He was also very proud of his father, a coal miner who rose to become superintendent of a very progressive coal company that set a high standard for safety." Tom Gish was "intensely proud," says son Ben, "that his father had invented the roof bolt, which probably saved more miners' lives than any other technological advance in the twentieth century." Ben says his father bristled when people criticized him as an anti-coal "outsider." "Anti-coal? No, he was as pro-coal as they come. He just wanted it done right."

Pat also had a background as a reporter in Kentucky, for the *Lexington Leader*. The couple hungered for a chance to put their skills to work in the hills and hollows of their beloved Appalachia. When the Gishes bought the *Mountain Eagle* in 1956, it was a fairly bland publication, with a masthead that read, "A Friendly Non-Partisan Weekly Newspaper Published Every Thursday."

The first thing the Gishes did was change the slogan to "The Mountain Eagle: It Screams." And scream it did, taking on unsafe coal mines, strip-mining devastation, poverty, inferior schools, and corrupt public officials. Not that they set out to be crusaders. "We could have been an establishment paper," Tom Gish once told author Studs Terkel. "We sometimes wonder what would have happened had the establishment, instead of opposing us, co-opted and embraced us."

Fat chance. In the early days of their coverage, the Gishes discovered that public business in Letcher County was not, in fact, conducted publicly. But they insisted on reporting what went on at, say, the county school board, even if it meant they had to stand in a corner because no chair would be provided for outsiders. (Laurie Ezzell would recognize that trick.) The school board and other agencies responded to this pushy behavior by passing a resolution saying press coverage was not permitted, an outrage that prompted more editorials in the *Eagle*. "The

Mountain Eagle and its editors and reporters," wrote Gish on one occasion, "take seriously their obligation to report the news. The *Eagle* will not be pushed aside without all the screaming and clawing the old bird can muster." The relentless insistence on access eventually led to Kentucky's first open public meeting law.

Such progress had a high personal price. According to the IRJCI's Rudy Abramson, "the doctor who delivered Tom Gish into the world was the school board chairman and the political boss of Letcher County, and he put out the word that school board employees were not to buy the *Mountain Eagle*. Along Main Street in Whitesburg, word was spread that Tom was a Communist. The *Eagle* lost for all time its major advertiser, an automobile dealer, which had been largely responsible for keeping the paper's books in the black."

At one point, boycotts by some readers and advertisers meant the paper was reduced to just four tabloid pages. The whole family, including the five kids, pitched in to get the paper out during hard times. "We had to do it all," remembers Ben Gish. "Since I was old enough to function, we were put to work, folding pages, putting in the inserts, delivering the papers. I literally slept on mailbags at the office."

But the Gishes never wavered. Despite the boycotts and even death threats, they stayed in Whitesburg. When asked by Charles Kuralt in 1969 why he insisted on staying, Tom Gish chuckled and said, "That would amount to a kind of surrendering that I just can't do."

They also got some help from an unexpected source, remembers Bethell, who worked long hours as an unpaid reporter for the *Mountain Eagle* in the '60s, whenever he could steal time away from his federal job supervising VISTA volunteers. "During the advertising boycotts," Bethell notes, "a man by the name of

Ray Collins would take out full page ads to keep them afloat." Collins was the owner of a Royal Crown Cola bottling company in the county. He disagreed with the Gishes on a number of issues, Bethell recalls, but "he was a person of real principle and he thought the Gishes were brave people. He admired them, and that was that." The Gishes named their youngest son Ray in his honor.

But even without that fortuitous patronage, the Gishes would have found a way to stick with it. For one thing, they were incredibly stubborn. "Tom was mild-mannered," says Bethell, "until you got on his bad side. Then there was no appeal. If he had been crossed by someone, he would bring them down."

In addition to that personal stubborn streak, the Gishes were sharply attuned to signs of injustice and—as the old journalism adage goes—a need to "to comfort the afflicted and afflict the comfortable." Tom Gish was outraged at the poverty he saw all around him. In 1983 he told NPR's Noah Adams about just one example he witnessed: "A woman came in [to the *Mountain Eagle* office] asking for two dollars. This was before Medicaid or Medicare. It was about the worst stench I've ever come across from a person." The woman had diabetes and gangrene, and "her leg was literally rotting off. She was without medical care. She was out on the streets of a Kentucky town in the United States of America, begging for funds to get medical treatment." The woman eventually died without getting the care she needed.

That moment served as a true epiphany for Gish. Readers of the *Mountain Eagle* learned not only about the failure of government to help in such cases but also about situations in which government action made things worse. The *Mountain Eagle* was one of the first news organizations to point out that coal companies were destroying the environment through strip mining, often to fulfill federal Tennessee Valley Authority contracts. In a 1960 editorial, Tom Gish wrote, "The greatest of all threats to our native beauty and our potential as a tourist center is in the fledgling strip coal mine industry, which threatens almost overnight to turn our mountains into denuded hunks of rock looking as if they were created by Hollywood for a special horror movie."

Harry Caudill, author of *Night Comes to the Cumberlands* and a friend of Tom Gish, told NPR: "He was a mighty lonely voice, pointing out that these hills were being destroyed and that the destruction of the hills meant the destruction of the water and when you destroy the physical environment, the people will have to leave. And I think the little *Mountain Eagle* had a very considerable influence in bringing about ultimately the federal strip mining law."

The publication of Caudill's book and the relentless reporting of the *Eagle* got the attention of the national press. In addition to visits by Kuralt and other network correspondents, veteran *New York Times* reporter Homer Bigart came to investigate the Gishes' reports about the dire poverty of Appalachia. "At first, he was skeptical," Tom Gish recalled later. "So he went out and talked to people all over the county and then he came back to the office and told us that everything we'd said was absolutely true. If anything, he said, we'd understated the problem."

Bigart's front-page articles in the *New York Times* caught the attention of the White House, which eventually led to President Johnson's announcement of an "unconditional" war on poverty. Actually, it was never unconditional enough to suit the Gishes, and the *Eagle* continued to call for more action. In one 1964 editorial, Gish wrote, "We sadly fear . . . that President Johnson, in formulating his Appalachian program, has listened to the men of little courage in Frankfort [Kentucky] and Washington who run in terror at the mention of public power and who instead of true development would give eastern Kentucky another decade of planning and talking."

Even so, Gish had focused national attention on Appalachia's dire situation. Eventually all the reporters who visited the area knew to go to the *Eagle* first for information and tips. The heightened attention on the area created resentment among many locals and triggered even more threats against the Gish family and the paper's reporters.

"I remember very well," Bethell says, "walking down the street of Whitesburg and seeing people cross to the other side to avoid you." But that was in town, he adds. Out in the rest of the county, up in the hollows, people loved the *Eagle* because it stood up for their interests. Nevertheless, "there was a lot of thuggery in those days": "When you drove on mountain roads at night, you always had one eye on the rearview mirror." Pat Gish felt some guilt about having the kids sleep on the floor of the office when they were getting the paper out, Bethell notes, but she was afraid to leave them at home.

Ben Gish says his parents never told him about the more serious death threats until he was older. "My parents always hid that stuff from us," he explains. Still, he tells me that his older sisters received the brunt of the local backlash when they were in school, mostly because their friends' parents were all in the coal business. "My problems," he recalls, "didn't come until high school and that was mostly from pissed-off teachers who would make nasty little quips about the paper."

But nothing quite matched the horror of Ben's seventeenth year, when an arsonist burned down the offices of the *Mountain Eagle*. The firebombing came after Tom Gish had printed a series of editorials criticizing the local police for harassing young people in town and for violating their constitutional rights. "If you are a teenage boy out in a car at night, you can expect to be followed, stopped, searched, cussed out, and generally harassed by our local officers," wrote Gish at the time. "It is a crime to be a teenager in Letcher County."

Ben Gish was among the teenagers targeted by that harassment, and it was about to get worse. "That was a bad year for me," he says. "That July, my girlfriend got killed in a car wreck. Then a month later, the paper burned."

Ben says his parents were out of town at the time. When he and his siblings heard the wail of the fire siren calling volunteers to report, they did what the Gish kids were trained to do: they called and asked where the fire was. Told it was at the *Mountain Eagle* offices, they ran down to the building to watch as the family business went up in flames. "It was the next day before we could get in touch with our parents," he remembers. "They never cried or anything. I'm sure they were angry, but dad was just too stubborn to quit."

The Gishes rallied to put the paper out the following week, working on old-fashioned typewriters at their house. And in a gesture of defiance to the arsonists, they changed the slogan to "The Mountain Eagle: It STILL Screams."

The police then came to their home and accused Ben of starting the fire, saying he had been smoking pot at the office. "I agreed to take a lie detector test," he says, "something I would never do today." He passed the test and went off to college. A subsequent arson investigation discovered that coal operators had paid a Whitesburg city policeman to have the newspaper office torched. Although that cop was convicted, he was given a one-year suspended sentence. And he flaunted the fact that he had basically gotten away with it, driving a car with a vanity plate that read "EAGLEBURNER." He even ran for the office of county jailer and handed out matchbooks with his name on them during the campaign. Ben Gish finds some satisfaction in the fact that the guy was "trounced at the polls."

Through it all, the Gish family stuck it out. Bill Bishop, a journalist who worked at the *Mountain Eagle* right after he got out of college in 1975, is still amazed at their tenacity. "That they made it as long as they did . . . ," he tells me with a mixture of admiration and amazement, having no need to finish the thought. Bishop, who went on to report for the *Austin Statesman* and now runs a rural news site with his wife called dailyyonder.com, says the *Mountain Eagle* attracted a lot of good young reporters who were not afraid to work very long hours. "There were no days off, because after working all night to get the paper out each week, we would have to stuff inserts the next morning, load our cars with papers, and deliver them. All for minimum wage." But no one complained, he notes, because the Gishes worked even harder. After Pat worked all night to get the paper out, she would get on a bus to Louisville each week to take classes at the university there. She was working toward a master's degree that would allow her to open a housing agency for the poor. She did all of this in addition to getting the paper out and raising five kids. And the kicker, says Bishop, is that her weekly bus trip was five hours long. Each way.

So no one complained about overwork. And every new reporter started the same way, typing up "community columns," articles by local folks about local events. As Bishop puts it, "These were essentially blogs written in people's own voices." When the Gishes first bought the paper, they eliminated this particular feature, and circulation collapsed. So they reinstated the columns and instructed new reporters to publish them verbatim. "These people," says Bishop, "had a voice that would be ruined if you monkeyed with their style."

In the 1980s they expanded the concept of "community columns" with a feature they called "Speak Your Piece," which allowed people to express their opinions without signing their names. In the hollows and hills of Appalachia, old family grudges tend to stick, and speaking out against the two biggest employers—coal companies and the county schools—could be risky in a place where unemployment stood as high as 37 percent. "Speak Your Piece" gave people an outlet that did not necessarily encourage personal vendettas. Which means some of the best stuff is, in fact, deeply personal. One woman wrote simply, "To my husband's mistress—I know who you are." Some blow the whistle on a neighbor: "How do people on the head of Cumberland River keep foster children and keep three big dogs in the house and 14, 15, cats and dogs tied outside? Somebody isn't doing their job. That ought to be checked on." And in almost every issue, haikus of heartbreak: "I think it is a shame for a guy to propose to a girl and hide it from his parents. Then he acts like she is trash."

When the Gishes added "Speak Your Piece" to the paper, Bishop remembers, "circulation really jumped among young people" because they felt safe to express themselves. Sure enough, in the "Speak Your Piece" column from an issue featuring a front-page story about the school board's demotion of a popular middle school principal, there were a number of entries from students—anonymous, of course—who expressed outrage at the demotion. "I am a student at Jenkins Middle-High School," wrote one. "We want our principal back. I don't have a good home life and Mrs. Bentley truly cares about each student up there. It doesn't matter if you're poor, rich, smart, or special ed., she treats everyone equally and with respect. We miss you and we will get you back. Don't let us down, Mrs. Bentley. Fight for what is right. You are not alone."

Bishop says the whole idea of "Speak Your Piece" is rooted in Tom Gish's respect for his readers. "You know how you hear that condescending phrase in newsrooms," he tells me, "when editors ask 'what would the average reader want?' Well, Tom would turn red when he heard that phrase. 'There is no average reader,' he would tell his staff, 'don't ever think you know more than the people who read the *Eagle*, because you don't. No one is better than a reader of the *Mountain Eagle!*' He had the ultimate respect for his readers."

In addition to the "Speak Your Piece" feature and the community columns, Tom Gish told NPR, he made sure people heard about "who's visiting, who's quilting, whatever's interesting." One popular feature was a page full of Thanksgiving recipes by children, including this one for turkey: "Directions: Kill it. Take it home and put it in a pan to cook. Put ketchup, noodles, and chocolate chips on it. Bake it for 7 minutes at 68 degrees. Cut it in half and eat it."

It was that delightful attention to detail that made so many people feel as though the *Mountain Eagle* was their paper, even when the editorials were taking dangerous stands against powerful interests in the county. As Bethell put it in the IRJCI tribute to the Gishes: "They have produced week after week . . . a living, breathing, working definition of what good rural journalism is all about. They have always paid close attention to what could be described, wrongly, as the small stuff. In the pages of the *Eagle* you can count on knowing when the redbuds are blossoming and how the mist looks on Pine Mountain, who has come home for the holidays, who owes back taxes, and who has died."

That sort of relentless outpouring of news items large and small, provocative and personal, takes a huge toll. And just as the Ezzell family paid the price, so too did the Gish family.

"We never had any money," says Ben Gish, "but we didn't know any better, because everybody was poor." His parents would accept clothes and shoes for the children in trade for advertising, he says, and "a '53 Chevy Bel Air is the only car I can remember. It had holes in the floorboard so that you could see the road flash by underneath." Just like the Ezzell family, the Gishes never had a true family vacation, although "we got to go to Toronto once for a few days." A couple of Ben's siblings left Whitesburg, but a few have decided to make it their home, including a sister who went to Yale for a medical degree. Ben says he can't imagine doing anything but editing the *Mountain Eagle*; "It's all I know," he says. He splits his time between the paper, which is still a seven-days-a-week job, and caring for his mother, Pat, who lives next door.

These days, says Ben, multinational corporations control the coal industry, and they can't really organize a local boycott of the newspaper. The big story now, he notes, is the drilling for natural gas. "They're really tearin' up jack," he tells me, adding, "you're likely to get run off the road by Halliburton trucks." The problem, he says, is the use of hydraulic "fracking" to open up gas deposits, a process that some environmentalists believe leads to water pollution and seismic instability. According to Gish, folks worry about this because of the unstable earth in the region. In the town of Jenkins, for example, a number of people were killed when a water tank toppled onto some homes. Among the dead was an elderly man who had been sitting on his porch listening to the radio. After the water tank was replaced, the gas company started drilling and fracking at the site of the new tank. "Families of the deceased," Gish says, "were freaking out, actually in tears."

And Ben Gish was there to tell their story. He also writes about the horrors of addiction to OxyContin, the "hillbilly heroin." And there is never a dearth of bad politicians offering up new material. Not long ago, the *Mountain Eagle* wrote an article about a man running for the position of county judge. Gish says he was putting out misleading ads about the incumbent, "who happened to be one of the best county judges we ever had." Just before the election, on the day the *Eagle* came out with an article exposing the lies in those ads, Gish recounts, the "bad guy" had his cronies go out and steal all the papers from the newsstands and stores. He went on to win a very narrow victory. A number of readers told Ben Gish they would have voted the other way if they had read the article exposing the false advertising.

The *Mountain Eagle* screamed about that, too.

After Tom Gish retired because of ill health, says Bethell, "we had some all-night talks in his hospital room." There was plenty of time, at last, for reflection, something of a luxury for someone who had been pumping out a paper every week for fifty years. And the Big Question finally came up: "Did it make a difference?"

Bethell does not sentimentalize. "Did we stop the scourge of strip mining? No. Does eastern Kentucky have a great educational system? No. But there are so many things you cannot trace when it comes to the impact of the *Eagle*."

Tom Gish, he says, answered the question *with* a question.

"What was the alternative?"

When Tom Gish died, Bethell left his home in Washington DC and headed for Whitesburg to help Ben put out a special edition of the paper. The headline of the front-page obituary read simply, "Tom Gish, Newspaperman." The front page also featured an editorial cartoon depicting an eagle clutching a copy of the newspaper; the words "it screams" had been crossed out and replaced by "it mourns." The special edition contained impassioned remembrances from many of the reporters who had worked for Tom Gish over the years.

From Sam Adams: "Over the years, reporters for the *Mountain Eagle* have been threatened, harassed, prosecuted, and even beaten. When I went to work there in 1986, right out of college, Pat's advice was: 'If anyone doesn't like what you've written, tell them you're sorry they feel that way and walk away.' Tom's advice: 'Tell them to go to hell.'"

From Helen Winternitz: "I saw Tom get the truth out in more than one way. During the gruesome disaster when the Scotia Mine near Whitesburg exploded twice in 1976, killing twenty-six, the *Eagle* was the first to get the story: the mine owner had scrimped on ventilation, allowing lethal concentrations of methane gas to build up underground. We had the story, but before we went to press Tom shared it with the flock of big-daily reporters who had descended on Whitesburg. He didn't care who scooped whom. He invited the reporters to the *Eagle*'s cramped office, where the paper's small and intense staff was laying the paper's pages, and let them all read our coverage and take what they wanted. And he also had an entire roasted turkey brought in to feed his fellow journalists as they pursued what he hoped would be the truth."

From Phil Primack: "Early on, after Tom heard my interview with someone, he said I'd asked the right questions and treated the subject respectfully. 'Just one thing,' he said, reaching for the white-out fluid we used back in those days to fix our flawed typewritten copy. 'You're from the North, and you all talk kind of fast. Around here, when someone pauses, it's often meant to be a semi-colon, not a period.' [The lesson:] Have the patience to wait through the pause—something memorable might follow. He was so right."

Another journalist who knew how to wait through the pause and elicit something memorable was Charles Kuralt, whose piece about the Gishes on the CBS Evening News in 1969 is still worth a dust-off. In the black and white film (no videotape yet), we see Pat and Tom Gish and all five children hard at work getting the paper out on a Thursday morning, and we hear Tom Gish talk about one of his reporters being threatened by coal company goons. Then, over the clickety-clack of the newspaper rolling off the press, Kuralt's sonorous bass voice gets to the heart of the matter: "It is what is known as freedom of the press—that one man with a typewriter and an offset printing machine may take on any giant."

Kuralt is gone. Tom Gish is gone. The offset printing machine is gone. But the courage "to take on any giant" lives on. Just ask Ben Gish.

The *Mountain Eagle* still screams.

CHAPTER THREE

Curmudgeons

Curmudgeons are simply crusaders with attitude. They tend to be cranky when those in power abuse their authority, pugnacious when defending the abused, and indefatigable when giving a voice to the voiceless. And they don't care who they piss off.

Seventy-year-old Bruce Anderson is a curmudgeon in the most honorable sense of the word. "Righting wrongs" trumps "being liked" every time. "Things have gone terribly awry," he says, "and ordinary people, unrepresented people—and that's most of us—really don't have a weapon, don't have any kind of a voice. A lot of the big newspapers do some great reporting, but out in the outback here, it's pretty rare."

Owner and editor of the *Anderson Valley Advertiser* (known locally as the AVA) in Mendocino County, California, Anderson is notorious for pissing off the powers that be, political leanings be damned. "The country weekly that tells it like it is!" is one of the mottos on the front page, along with "Fanning the Flames of Discontent" and a quote from Joseph Pulitzer, "Newspapers should have no friends."

Even so, Anderson has plenty of admirers, including *Nation* columnist and media critic Alexander Cockburn, who lives in nearby Humboldt County and is a contributing columnist to the AVA. He calls it "the best small newspaper in America" and "an example of all that is seditious, muckraking, contrarian, courageous, and uproarious in American journalism." Bruce Anderson's work, he says, is "up there with the best of Paine, Twain, Steffens, and H. L. Mencken."

Anderson laughs loudly when I ask him about the comparison to Mencken. "No," he says, "Mencken was a lot smarter than I am, a lot better writer." Still, he admits that it is nice to get such a compliment from his friend Cockburn, "one of the foremost polemicists."

I met Anderson—a large man sporting a full beard—in his small office above a store in Boonville, a town of about a thousand people in the heart of Anderson Valley. The three-hour drive from San Francisco—through verdant rolling hills of apple orchards and California oaks, ancient stands of redwoods, misty coastlines, and vineyards out of Tuscany—was the geological and cultural antithesis of the dry, flat trek through the Texas Panhandle. Anderson Valley (the name has no connection to its irascible newspaperman) is a lush sliver of land nestled between two coastal mountain ranges—what the fictional Brigadoon might look like if it were bathed in a marijuana haze.

"Mendocino," Anderson says, "is the intoxicant capital of the world." The county's perfect growing conditions for marijuana have made the plant its number one export crop and attracted both small-time cultivators and Mexican criminal syndicates. Every edition of the AVA gives some indication of this reality. "Aggressive Cannabis Defense!" claims one of several ads for "pot" lawyers in the area. And then there's the sheriff's log:

7/28 4:28 p.m. A caller said it was "possible" that marijuana was thriving in an area off Highway 128 outside of Yorkville. The probability factor of marijuana growing anywhere in the Anderson Valley at this time of year is roughly 98%.

That last bit of sarcasm came, of course, from the editor, not the sheriff. Anderson is often critical of local law enforcement's tendency to go after the "low-hanging fruit," small growers who are raising more than the six plants now allowed under a local statute, and not the big criminals—the syndicate guys, armed and very dangerous, who are raising huge (and illegal) amounts of marijuana in the hills. (In Mendocino County, the question is not whether citizens can grow pot at all but *how* much they can grow.) Anderson regularly reminds readers of the violent crime associated with the more nefarious types involved in this illegal activity. As he wrote in a "Valley People" column from September 10, 2008,"Most county residents are aware of the vicious home invasion robberies which recently occurred north of Fort Bragg. One of those left one man nearly dead from a gratuitous beating, the other featured a blow torch held to the genitals of a man slow to inform the robbers of the location of other marijuana enterprises."

But marijuana is not the only intoxicant making news in the AVA. Anderson is not afraid to go after the wineries when he hears they are dumping pesticides, guzzling more than their share of water, or exploiting labor. And he takes aim at bigger newspapers for ignoring the story. "The big media around here, you know, they're on the take from the wine industry," he tells me. "I mean, they have whole 'wine sections,' and you know they're getting cases and cases of free wine." He constantly picks on the local congressman, Mike Thompson, for allegedly (my word, not his) being in the pocket of the wine interests. A one-line reference in the AVA to an election said simply, "By the time you read this, Mike Thompson will have been reelected to represent the wine industry in Congress."

Many of the wineries are the property of wealthy newcomers who live in mansions built on the ridgeline overlooking Anderson Valley. Anderson refers to these folks as "hill muffins" and "the Golden Horde." These are not off-but on-the-record references, mind you. Not that his scorn discriminates: right-wing ranchers are the "rural fascist league," and environmentalists and revolutionaries are "self-appointed righteous ones." There is "a lot" of "lotus-eating, lazy mysticism" around here, he tells me.

Curmudgeons of the Bruce Anderson variety are equal-opportunity town criers when it comes to pointing out that the emperor *du jour* has no clothes. Anderson himself is a paradox, "as courtly in person as he is caustic in print," according to a profile in the *Los Angeles Times*. He served in both the Marine Corps and the Peace Corps (where he met his wife, Ling). "I've always had a fairly sharp sense of injustice," he tells me, "and newspapers are a natural, I think, for people who want to do a little bit of good." And even his enemies, who are numerous, would have to agree with Anderson's assessment of the AVA's impact: "When people are going to do bad things, they have to look over their shoulder because we are here. And without it, they wouldn't."

Certainly, when Anderson bought the paper back in the '80s, no one was worried about an aggressive press. He and his wife were part of the hippie influx to the valley from San Francisco and had been operating a foster care facility. When the paper came on the market, he jumped at it. He immediately had a choice to make: "I can put out the paper that had existed, which was weekly tributes to bad people—you know, the chamber of commerce types," or hope that "people were sophisticated enough to want an honest paper about what was going in the county."

He took the circulation from 700 to today's 2,500, but many of those subscribers come from outside the area, some as far away as overseas diplomatic posts. He knew from the beginning that subscriptions and legal ads would be his primary source of funding. "I lost most of my advertisers right away," he laughs, "which is ironic, given the name of the paper." One former advertiser in Ukiah even sent him a telegram ("probably the last telegram sent in the U.S.," he chuckles, "since it had to be delivered by mail") saying simply, "OUT NOW!"

Anderson wasted no time in taking on the "bad people" at all levels of the social strata, and that often made him a personal target, especially in the early days when he and Ling printed the paper out of their house. "There was never any privacy, you know, never any down time. People would show up in the middle of the night, half-drunk and wanting to talk about something." It was not unusual for Anderson to chase off some of those people with one of the several guns he kept on the property. It was hardest on his wife, he says, because "she's not a rabble-rouser."

But rabble-rousing comes naturally to Anderson. At one meeting of the school board, the superintendent of schools called him "a tenth-ranked McCarthyite" for criticizing his agency, then got up and strode toward Anderson. "I thought he was going to attack me physically so I jumped up out of my chair and slugged him."

The district attorney charged Anderson with fifteen counts of disturbing the peace. He thought the charges were a tad excessive and a jury agreed, finding him guilty on only one count. Anderson was sentenced to thirty-five days in jail, something the authorities came to regret. While Anderson was in the county jail in Ukiah, he saw "grim, third-world conditions. Sheetrock is falling off the ceiling, guys were sleeping on the floor, showers wouldn't turn off, completely grim." So he organized the inmates and they filed a writ against the county. "The judge had to admit these conditions existed, and the county wound up building a whole new wing of the county jail."

"Actually," says Anderson as he leans back in his chair, smiling, "I was glad I went to jail on that one." Aside from getting a new jail built, the experience provided terrific material for the AVA.

And it hardly tempered his appetite for going after school administrators. In an October 2009 article headlined "The Chinks in the Superintendent's Niggardly Education," Anderson feasts on a platter of overcooked political correctness:

> It all started last March when Dennis Boaz, Ukiah teacher's rep, wrote to his union that Ukiah Unified had made only niggardly offers to teachers during union negotiations.
>
> Bryan Barrett, an assistant superintendent for the Ukiah Unified School District, was deeply offended by Boaz's communication.

The article then quotes Barrett's memo to the Ukiah Teachers' Association, which reads in part, "'Racism or suggested racism has absolutely no place in this district . . . and we have to question whether Mr. Boaz can continue as a spokesperson for teachers and for the negotiating team. His credibility and integrity are certainly at issue.'"

Anderson goes on to describe how Barrett took the issue to his superior.

> The scholarly Barrett . . . quickly enlisted the aggressive support of none other than the Mendocino County Superintendent

of Schools himself, Paul Tichinin, previously not known to rouse himself for anything other than raising, then defending, his annual compensation of some $120,000 for doing, well, whatever it is that Tichinin does.

Tichinin, cutting his usual two-hour lunch back to an austere ninety minutes, gathered his leadership team around him and, together, they crafted this emphatic message for Mr. George Young, California Teachers Association representative: "The words (Boaz) used were completely unacceptable. The comments are racially charged and show a complete lack of respect and integrity towards (*sic*) Dr. Nash, Ukiah Unified District Superintendent.'

Dr. Nash is black.

She hadn't complained because, it seems, alone among the school superintendents of Mendocino County, she knows that niggardly is not an ethnic slur.

Besides skewering the obvious and easy targets, Anderson has scored several investigative coups. When he discovered that local judges were using the county law library for their exclusive use despite the fact that county taxpayers were funding it, Anderson's relentless reporting won public access to the library. In the '90s he exposed an arson ring in Fort Bragg, which resulted in several arrests. "A couple of wealthy crooks burned down an old hotel and restaurant in the late '80s for the insurance," he recalls. His investigative series prompted some written death threats, and for a time Anderson carried a .38-caliber handgun for self-defense, although he says he was not all that worried. "When people want to kill you, they just kill you. They don't write letters telling you they will." But the alleged arsonists were never prosecuted because the statute of limitations ran out. Anderson blames the lack of an aggressive press in the Fort Bragg area for the belated investigation. "When the media falls down completely," he says, "we get George W. Bush at the national level and we get the hearts of towns being burned out" at the local level.

Curmudgeons hate bullies, and Bruce Anderson goes after them with a vengeance. When a Mendocino Indian named Bear Lincoln was accused of shooting a deputy in Round Valley in 1995, Anderson assigned one of his reporters, former logger and truck driver Mark Heimann, to the case. The AVA followed the story for three years, during which time they printed allegations that the police had roughed up the suspect's family and even pointed guns at the heads of children. They also reported that one of the deputies involved in the shootout that dark night on a lonely road had changed his story, and that photographs of the scene indicated that the shooting could not possibly have happened the way the police described it. The *Advertiser* began to speculate that Bear Lincoln might not be guilty but rather the victim of a police ambush.

Typical of Anderson, his reports of the case were not limited to the current facts as they unfolded; instead, they cited decades of Indian mistreatment in the area, something Anderson has researched rather exhaustively. As he wrote in his book *Mendocino Papers*, local Indian history could be summarized in a single sentence if you believed the historical account of one local museum: "Once upon a time a happy brown people lived in Mendocino County who were real good at making baskets, and then they weren't here any more."

Poring over historical documents from the 1800s, including depositions from those involved in the wholesale slaughter of thousands of Indians in the area, he learned that the first white settlers in the region were mostly criminals and outlaws who saw beautiful land for the taking and "weren't about to share it with those who had lived there for 12,000 years. . . . They shot Indian men where they found them, helped themselves to Indian women, sold Indian children into slavery, 'rez-ed' the Indians they hadn't managed to kill, indentured them, and segregated them for the next one hundred years."

The lingering remnants of that racism, Anderson believed, could easily lead to the railroading of an Indian for a crime he did not commit. So when Bear Lincoln wrote a letter to the AVA from jail, describing in his own words what had happened the night of the shooting, Anderson printed it in its entirety. And the authorities jumped on him. Anderson was jailed for refusing a court order to turn over the original letter to the Mendocino County District Attorney's Office, which wanted to use it as evidence in Lincoln's upcoming murder trial. When the judge told Anderson he would be placed in solitary confinement, isolated from other prisoners until he turned over the letter, Anderson joked to reporters, "I was at least hoping for an opportunity to explore my sexuality, and apparently even that last pleasure is being denied me."

He was finally released without ever "burning" the source that had delivered the copy of the letter. He had never had the original, as it turned out, something he could have told the judge to begin with. But then he would have lost the chance to attract more attention to the case, which he most certainly ended up doing. The Bear Lincoln trial received nationwide coverage due in no small part to the activity (critics would say the antics) of the *Anderson Valley Advertiser*.

In 1997 Bear Lincoln was acquitted of first- and second-degree murder. The jury hung 10 to 2 for acquittal on manslaughter. Lincoln was released after 26 months in jail.

Bruce Anderson continues to fight for those who otherwise would have no voice. When I visited him, he had just printed a front-page story headlined "Tree Rustling, Fort Bragg Style," which amounted to allegations by a property owner that her neighbors had cut down valuable (not to mention beautiful) redwood trees on her property while she was away. Not a very big deal, you might think, but that's because you don't think like Bruce Anderson.

"The big theme of that story is how this county too often works or doesn't work," he tells me. "Behind the scenes, the cops and the judges are all pals and there was no way this woman was going to get justice at the local level. NO WAY!"

And so he would have to see to it himself. His involvement began when the woman, Skye Nickell, brought several years' worth of files and documents on the case into his office. He figures that he put in fifty hours over several weeks determining exactly what had happened. "A lot of people," he notes, "cannot clearly tell their own story, so you operate like a cop and you keep going back over it, asking 'what happened here?'"

What happened, as he sees it, is that Ms. Nickell got screwed over by her neighbors the Cottrells, a law enforcement family with powerful pull in the county. Here is how Anderson began his story:

> The day after escrow closed on the Fort Bragg property Wayne and Mason Cottrell bought out on Franklin Road, they logged the property next door. Mason Cottrell is a Fort Bragg police officer. Mason's father is also a Coast police officer. You could say the Cottrells are a law enforcement family, not a logging family, but a few years ago, they did a little bit of both. The Cottrells said the big trees they took down on their neighbor's

property and made into lumber were on their side of the property line. They said they knew where the line was because a real estate agent [not a surveyor] had shown them the property lines.

Their neighbor, forty-one-year-old Skye Nickell, "was a single woman who was in Virginia when the Cottrells took eight trees from her property, trees valued at $53,200 but priceless to the lady who owned them."

Ms. Nickell managed to get a surveyor to confirm that the trees had been on her property, which might lead you to think the case was pretty much open and shut at that point.

Not by a long shot.

"Since that day, when she came home to find her trees gone, there's been six years of bullying lawyers, court appearances, depositions, lost files, judicial cowardice—all because a well-connected family of Fort Bragg, old-timers with a law-enforcement son and a law-enforcement in-law, stole the lady's trees."

Talking about the story in his office, Anderson gets riled up all over again. "I was angry. Clearly. Just one atrocity after another. Here's a tiny, single woman and they just figured they could do it to her and get away with it. Fortunately, she came up with a good lawyer at the end."

But, as it turned out, the end was nowhere in sight. Months after my visit to Boonville, I was still reading about the ongoing Tree Lady Saga in the AVA: "When the Cottrells discovered their big mistake, did they give Skye her logs back? No. The Cottrells sued the [now-dead] real estate agent's insurance company and got themselves another $23,500. Skye got nothing but a steady stream of abuse, much of it gratuitous, from the Cottrell's lawyer" (as well as a demand that she pay their legal fees).

And in yet another installment, rife with exasperation and barely concealed outrage:

In short, here's what happened to Skye's case: Mendocino County lost her case file. Twice. When it was finally found . . . Judge Jonathan Lehan said Skye's case was too old and threw it out. All this time, the Cottrells, the people who have twice profited from taking Skye's trees, have been represented by a Fort Bragg lawyer named John Ruprecht who once ran for District Attorney of Mendocino County. Mr. Ruprecht says Skye still owes him money for helping the Cottrells steal her trees. (If you recall Mr. Tulkinghorn from Dickens's great novel, *Bleak House*, you will instantly understand Mr. Ruprecht's ethical universe.) Mr. Ruprecht has grandly informed Skye that he'll settle with her for a $2,000 cashier's check. . . . Skye Nickell has recently been laid off from her job and doesn't have $2,000 for Mr. Tulkinghorn. Maybe the Cottrells will pay Tulkinghorn for Skye. After all, they have Skye's trees and they have the dead realtor's $23,500. They own the judge, too. They can afford to be magnanimous, one would think.

I think it's safe to say that if Ms. Nickell ever *sees* a nickel from this case, it will be due in large part to Bruce Anderson's wickedly literate and dogged coverage.

But for those who just like to snack on the AVA rather than indulge in the feasts of ongoing injustice, there are plenty of bully-bashing tidbits to nosh on. Consider this priceless piece from the "Off the Record" column:

Gary Bartlett, 56, of Point Arena, was booked into the County Jail last Friday for allegedly attempting to beat his son into the Army. The kid is 15. Bartlett, a surfer, is also known around town as Gun Gary, a kind of Point Arena bookend to the far more benign Bubble Bob, an urchin diver. Gun Gary apparently drinks to excess. The police report says Deputy Gander was summoned to the Bartlett home at 3 a.m. where young Bartlett told the deputy that Bartlett senior had become enraged when Bartlett junior informed him he wasn't interested in military service. Bartlett senior shoved the boy's head into a cabinet and later broke a stick over his head. When Mrs. Bartlett tried to keep her drunken husband away from the kid she got pushed around, too. Gun Gary's own military record is not known. What is known is that young people can't enlist until they're 18, by which time Bartlett junior ought to be able to defend himself against his demented father, who is now looking at charges of cruelty to a child, battery of a cohabitant (the unfortunate Mrs. Bartlett) and making terrorist threats.

Taking these kinds of digs at local residents leads to the occasional "demand" letters, as in "we demand you retract what you wrote or we will sue." "My approach to those," says Anderson, "is to say 'go ahead' and then reprint the provocation." He has rarely been sued in part, he suspects, because he doesn't have any money.

This is not to say he has never regretted something he wrote. In 1988 he pulled a stunt that attracted national attention, a mock interview with Doug Bosco, a local congressman. Anderson believed Bosco had sold out his environmental constituents on the issue of offshore drilling, so "we tried to smoke him out with this phony interview." In the satire, Anderson quoted Bosco as calling his green constituents "'a bunch of easily stirred-up, know-nothing malcontents who couldn't care less about anything other than their beautiful ocean and where their next joint is coming from.'"

Now most people, he says, "should get at that point that it's a parody, but they didn't!" He did not put a disclaimer on the article, he explains, because "other people's reading comprehension problems are not our responsibility." The wire services ran it, he continues, and "I thought it was funny as hell, because it showed how the media works, all picking up the story without checking."

But Congressman Bosco was not laughing. In fact, he threatened Anderson with a libel suit. That prompted another story in the AVA, this one about the threatened legal action:

> For his part, publisher Anderson seemed eerily delighted. "I will fight Bosco in the sushi bars, in his Tahoe condos, at the wine and cheese sips, in the BMW showrooms, and I'll sure as hell fight him in our nation's corrupt courtrooms. I don't like anything about the guy, beginning with his gutless, unprincipled politics. I also don't like his haircut, his house, his dog, or anything else about him."

Even though Anderson still laughs about the episode, he admits to feeling a tinge of regret. His enemies like to bring up the Bosco parody whenever they want to accuse of him of making stuff up. In retrospect, he concedes, it might have been one parody too far.

For all his curmudgeonly rants, Anderson believes strongly in providing space for opposing voices. The letters to the editor take up two to three pages each week, and he never edits them. He does respond to them, however, "when they are SO wrong," which can lead to months of back-and-forth in print. These letters, along with the articles by Anderson and a handful of reporters, help fill twelve pages each week. One of his reporters is Mark Scaramella, a retired Air Force officer who says he loves covering local politics. "I'm a connoisseur of tedium, I guess," he tells me. He gets paid next to nothing, but Anderson allows him all the column inches he wants. The resulting layout is never going to win any awards for design. There is "a lot of gray," admits Anderson, and few photos or ads to break up the monotony of the tiny nine-point type. Anderson says his daughter would hold the paper at arm's length and exclaim, "Ah, I'm bored already!"

But readers willing to dig through the layers of verbiage are often rewarded with marvelous stories. The AVA reminds me a bit of the opening scene in the movie *Blue Velvet*, in which the camera first focuses on the brilliant colors of a suburban lawn, pushes in closer and closer until the viewer is eye-level with the bugs beneath the lush green blades of grass, then moves right down to the muck beneath.

Bruce Anderson is a muckraker of the first order. He has great affection for the beautiful valley that accidentally shares his name, but he knows that there are always new secrets to be revealed. This is, after all, a place where early residents developed their own language, "Boontling," to confound outsiders. Some locals can still speak it, and tourists can pick up books about it. Much of the vocabulary revolves around residents' nicknames: breasts are known as "moldunes," after the nickname of one well-endowed valley woman; a pie is a "Charley Brown," the name of a farmer who ate pie with every meal; and a phone is called a "Walter" after the first person in the valley to get one.

The valley's geographic isolation has also provided a hide-out for various rough characters over the years. In the '60s, the Manson family spent some time here, and Jim Jones, who would eventually lead his cult members in a mass suicide in

Guyana, once taught sixth grade in the local school, even as he was developing his following. Slim Pickens, the actor, once called Boonville the toughest little town he ever visited.

Tough and tender, green and gritty—these are paradoxes that could easily define Anderson himself. His style of journalism is what modern bloggers might call "transparent," or what journalism schools might refer to as "advocacy journalism." Anderson doesn't care much for labels, but he tells me that "just the concept of objectivity is a false kind of goal. It leaves out our biases." Even so, he adds, "you've got to claim fairness. I mean, if you attack somebody or some institution, you're obligated to give them equal time."

Anderson also takes time to write about the people and events that have earned his affection over the years. In an article about the county fair, for example, his curmudgeon's mask slips off long enough for us to see why he sticks around these parts, despite his catalogue of complaints.

I like the Fair that first day, that Friday early afternoon when the flowers are still fresh, before the crowds become so thick it's hard to find old friends among all the strangers. . . . I noted a blue ribbon on Ann Fashauer's apple cake and made a note to beg one from her when I see her at Trivial Pursuit. Another Trivial Pursuit teammate, Barbara Scott, was in charge of the floral exhibits and the flowers never looked better, humbling to the writer whose dahlias seldom bloom and whose coreopsis never did show up this year.

Humbling? Anderson? And he grows *flowers*?

Many column inches later, he gets around to describing the parade, along with comments he hears from the crowd:

The Anderson Valley High School football team, as yet un-bloodied by actual gridiron combat, roared past with chest thumps and fierce roars. . . . Uncle Sam, a.k.a. Bruce Hering, passed by on a tractor and trailer with a bunch of children in it that said, "Buy Local," which caused me to wonder if the kids were (1) for sale and (2) organic. . . . The ever-ebullient Sheriff Allman brought up the rear, often stopping to leap from his command vehicle to shake hands with a constituent. Riding with the sheriff was a person in full clown costume, the juxtaposition prompting the inevitable, "Which one is the Sheriff?" And that was it, a most amusing little parade for the last best little fair in America.

Then he wrapped up the whole package with a paean more reminiscent of E. B. White than H. L. Mencken.

The Fair Days had been warm but not too warm, the nights cool but not too cool, and the Anderson Valley, sun-kissed and fog-blessed, was a happy place when the full moon rose up over Ukiah to chase the setting sun into the sea at Manchester. The 81st Fair had come and gone, and all was almost like it had always been in the Anderson Valley.

Almost. Anderson worries about this little slice of paradise. After *Forbes* magazine called it "the most undervalued beautiful place in America," Anderson feared for its future. "It's now run by millionaire lawyers with 10 acres of grapes," he told his friend Alexander Cockburn, "and their own silly faces on their wine labels."

But on the day I spoke with him, Anderson vowed to stick around to keep an eye on those millionaires, not to mention all the miscreants who provide him with weekly skewering material.

"My energy levels have been described as fiendish," he laughs, "and I will do this indefinitely, until I drop."

Bruce Anderson has never met Jim Stiles, the publisher of the *Canyon Country Zephyr* in southern Utah. Which is a shame, really, because when it comes to curmudgeon status, these two share the top tier. In the words of one fan, "Jim Stiles is the rock in the boot, the burr under the saddle blanket, the leak in the inner tube. We who love the West ignore him at our peril."

The *High Country News* (HCN) refers to him as "the West's curmudgeon-in-chief ('All the news that causes fits' is his motto)." He put out the bimonthly *Zephyr* in print form for twenty years, and now he publishes it online—increasing the content and adding color photography—at canyoncountryzephyr.com. But more on that in a moment.

His latest rant, says HCN, can be summed up as "the super-rich make really rotten environmental stewards." More on that in a moment as well.

The point is that Stiles falls so clearly in the curmudgeon category that it is hard to imagine anyone disputing it, especially Stiles himself.

"Oh, no," he groans when I mention the unofficial title. "Not the curmudgeon thing again. Could you at least call me 'a cuddly curmudgeon?'"

This is an odd request from someone whose paper bears the slogan, "Clinging Hopelessly to the Past" and who sees his mission as "documenting the death of the West I love." As Stiles wrote, "When I started *The Zephyr*, I had to make a choice that I didn't even realize when I made it. I could either be honest (to my own values, at least), even painfully blunt, or I could try to be liked. My ornery personality probably made that decision for me."

To his adversaries, he is about as cuddly as a porcupine. But sitting across from him in his cozy Monticello, Utah, home, surrounded by his beloved cats, I could make a case for "cuddly." While Stiles is nearly sixty years old, he exudes the boyish charm and fitness of someone much younger. And, like Anderson, his love affair with an especially beautiful place, and his righteous anger at those who would destroy it, are the driving forces behind his outspoken (some might say obstreperous) advocacy. His single-minded passion *could* be seen as endearing if, of course, you happen to agree with him.

Stiles moved to Moab, Utah, in the mid-1970s after reading Edward Abbey's *Desert Solitaire*, which accomplished for the Four Corners region of the Southwest what Thoreau did for Walden Pond. The towering red rock formations and slick rock canyons, set against a sky of heart-stopping blue, inspired Abbey to write, "For the first time, I felt I was getting close to the West of my deepest imaginings, the place where the tangible and mythical became the same." Abbey took a job as a backcountry ranger at Arches National Park, even as he attacked the development in the national parks as "industrial tourism" that would lead to "national parking lots." He aggravated people from all political spectrums, including ranchers, land developers, and environmentalists. He was, in fact, a living preview of Jim Stiles.

Stiles eventually met and befriended Abbey, and he even followed his career path of working as a ranger at Arches before turning to writing. Like Abbey, he worships at the church of "Leave the West Alone." "*Desert Solitaire*," he says, "was my holy book." He created the *Zephyr* by convincing a hundred of his friends and family to buy a ten-dollar subscription and by persuading some advertisers to sign up in advance. Abbey even promised to write an article for the debut issue.

On the launch date of March 14, 1989, Stiles drove to Cortez, Colorado, where the first issue of the *Zephyr* was coming off the press. As he drove back to Moab with two thousand copies of his new paper, Stiles writes in his book *Brave New West*, "I wondered what Abbey would think of it. I had just shut off the motor and was unloading the first bundle when a friend approached and asked if I'd heard about Abbey."

His mentor had died just hours before the first issue of the *Zephyr* was printed.

"It seemed like the strongest voice in the American West had been silenced on the day that I tried to start this little voice," Stiles later told documentary filmmakers Doug Haws-Davis and Drury Gunn Carr. "It's always hard for me to believe that Abbey never saw one issue of this paper. Because he always seems a part of every issue I've put together."

That influence has never been subtle. As journalist John Fayhee wrote in the *High Country News*, "Though it would be unfair to call the *Zephyr* the official publication of Abbey's memory, it would not be too much a stretch to call it a channeling device for his philosophy."

Abbey's philosophy might best be described as "don't mess with paradise," and given the track record of humankind dating back to Adam and Eve, believers are bound to be disappointed. No wonder, then, that Stiles seems to live in a state of perpetual dissatisfaction. Still, he feels a Cassandra-like urge to keep telling uncomfortable truths. As he describes this paradoxical combination of passion and despair, "I'm all fired up with no expectations."

But he didn't start out that way. At first, the *Zephyr* was fashioned as an alternative voice in Moab, not as a screed. "Every month," says Stiles, "I interviewed the county commissioners and the mayor." But he soon learned that "you can write thirty stories they agree with, but write one they don't like and they hate you for the rest of your life."

One they did not like came in 1992, when Stiles revealed that the commissioners had established a new highway commission without the consent of voters and then appointed themselves to run that commission, which gave them access to all sorts of state funding. The commissioners would have used the funding to build a highway from Vernal to Moab across pristine desert cliffs, mostly for the benefit of the oil and gas industries. Stiles used the *Zephyr* to bring out the facts about the proposed highway and, more important, to push a petition drive that changed the way the county elected its local representatives. The highway was never built, and the new election procedure ushered in a more responsive county government.

It took little time for Stiles to morph from a crusader into a curmudgeon, one who welcomed an honest fight over principles. In fact, much of his frustration these days comes from his inability to prod his latest targets into an open debate. "When former Grand County commissioner Jimmie Walker said he could sum up the *Zephyr* in one word—'shit'—I had no idea then how grateful I would be years later for such candor."

Even the competition, the family-owned (and relatively conservative) *Moab Times-Independent*, conceded that Stiles brought an important new voice to coverage of the area. Sam and Adrien Taylor have published their weekly for more than fifty years. "I thought [the *Zephyr*] was a fine publication," Sam Taylor told *High Country News*, "though Jim and I did not always agree on the issues." His wife is not as complimentary. "We call his rag the alternative newspaper," she tells me. "He doesn't carry news, he writes opinions. We reserve our editorials for the editorial page."

When I spoke with Adrien, she was still smarting from Stiles's caricature of her in a skimpy bikini in the *Zephyr*. When she complained, she says, he refused to apologize. She concluded from this encounter "that you don't get into a pissing match with a skunk." The "cuddly" adjective never came up. "I don't have a lot of use for Jim," she says, adding that she does not consider him "that fine of an artist."

Adrien Taylor may have taken offense at Stiles's artistic rendering, but she seems to be in the minority. His caricatures are widely admired, and Abbey once asked him to illustrate all his books. Stiles draws every illustration in the *Zephyr*, including amusing images of those who place ads with him. "Jim appeals to their egos," remarked the editor of a paper in Monticello, in grudging admiration for the way Stiles could pull in advertisers from businesses he would criticize in print—real estate, for example.

"When you're cartooning someone who's paying you," says Stiles in the documentary version of *Brave New West*, "you probably should not accentuate their flaws." But caricature is all about exaggeration, of course, and once the advertisers realized that their cartoon faces attracted more people to their ads, they were willing participants. "It's the only paper I know where some people tell me they read the ads before the stories."

That personalized approach, in fact, seems to bring out the inner artist in the advertisers. In one reader-submitted issue of the *Zephyr* dedicated to "Perfect Moments," even the advertisers got into the curmudgeonly tone. Gene Schafer's automotive repair ad, for example, read, "A perfect moment? I'll give you a perfect moment: when somebody's car breaks down and they can fix it themselves, instead of knocking on my goddamn door at 3 o'clock in the morning." The ad lists his location as "somewhere in Monticello, Utah," his phone as "look it up yourself," and his Web site as "you gotta be kidding me."

The "Perfect Moments" issue prompted some readers to wonder if Stiles had lost his ironic edge and wandered into treacle territory. Not so. A friend asked him in print, "What the hell are you talking about? 'Perfect moments.' In the *Zephyr*! Are you insane? Who are you?" He answered: "It's still me, your lovable little buddy and fellow curmudgeon. . . . What I hoped my little survey would prove (and it did) was that when all of us truly consider the times in our lives that we treasure the most, those moments rarely have anything to do with accumulation of physical wealth or the flaunting display of our 'stuff.'"

Antimaterialism is a consistent theme of the *Zephyr*: Stiles battles the forces of what he calls "rich-weasel greedhead stupidity." But over the years, Stiles began to realize that greed could pop up in unexpected places, forcing him to alter his strategy and causing old allies to abandon him as they suddenly found themselves in the curmudgeon's crosshairs.

When Stiles first started the *Zephyr*, he went after the traditional foes of environmentalists—the so-called extractive industries of timber and uranium as well as any ranchers who allowed their cows to overgraze the land and destroy the streams. Environmental groups loved him, cheering when he successfully battled a toxic-waste incinerator proposed for Moab in the 1980s.

Then, in the '90s, Stiles had an uncomfortable epiphany. The gradual failure of the local extractive industries had created an economic vacuum that the "amenities economy" would fill. In a 1993 piece in the *Zephyr* called "New West Blues," he wrote, "We are watching, in effect, the West's last land rush, and when it's over the West will bear little resemblance to what it is today." Moab once again became a boomtown, only now it was not uranium miners flocking to the area but tourists—hordes of Jeep aficionados in search of challenging terrain to conquer, packs of mountain bikers, decked out in Lycra, heading to the now-famous Slick Rock Trail. And land speculators galore. "More than 60 percent of the homes and structures are now owned by people who do not live here," Stiles tells me. Moab, once "a funky little town" where everyone knew everyone, he says, became the home of motels, souvenir shops, "adventure tour" promoters, and fast food outlets that transformed Main Street. McDonald's came to town and McMansions came to the wilderness. Condos sprouted like mushrooms and—to Stiles—seemed just as unnatural in this fragile desert environment.

He was horrified. The vacuum left by the declining extractive industries and cattle ranching, a vacuum he had helped bring about, had been filled with what Edward Abbey called "the forces of industrial tourism."

And so Stiles reloaded and took aim at some of the very same people who had long supported him: environmentalists.

Not that he is accusing environmental groups of purposely creating the amenities-based tourist onslaught. But Stiles says some groups, like the Southern Utah Wilderness Alliance (SUWA), are complicit because they are afraid to criticize all those millions of tourists who are going to love the wilderness to death. Moab is now known as the mountain biking capital of the world, attracting five hundred to a thousand cyclists for its annual Fat Tire rally. If you want to camp in Arches these days, you have to book a reservation at least a year in advance.

"When millions of people all go to the same place to try to find 'solitude,'" Stiles told a radio interviewer, "they're not going to find it, eventually. When Moab got cachet, we were doomed." None of the major environmental organizations, he says, expressed concern. "It was as if they didn't even notice all the hundreds of thousands of people coming in and riding their mountain bikes through cryptobiotic [environmentally fragile] soil."

This new rant by the West's curmudgeon-in-chief took a lot of readers by surprise. Suddenly the *Zephyr* was aiming its barbs at the proponents of "the New West." One issue was headlined: "Old West versus New West, Cows versus Condos: the Similarities are Striking." In *Brave New West*, Stiles writes, "Most Old Westerners oppose wilderness because they believe it will limit their access to public lands. Sometimes their physical abuse of the land itself is dramatic and the damage is long term. But Old Westerners understand one key component of wilderness far better than their adversaries. They understand solitude, quiet, serenity, the emptiness of the rural West. They *like* the emptiness."

"New Westerners," he continues, "are individually more sensitive to the resource but are terrified of solitude. They'll walk around cryptobiotic crust, but leave them alone in the canyons without a cell phone and a group of companions and they'd be lost, both physically and metaphysically. Because New Westerners need to travel in packs, the collective resource damage is far more than they might realize."

Stiles rails against SUWA and other environmental groups for what he sees as their hypocrisy in this area: their willingness to criticize ranchers and ATV riders, for example, but not the realtors and mountain bikers. And he is not afraid to go after the big names in the environmental movement, including a wealthy SUWA contributor named David Bonderman. "No one dares to question him," says Stiles, even though Bonderman "is building a fifteen thousand square foot home in Moab to supplement his thirteen thousand square foot home in Aspen."

Needless to say, this shift in targets has not always sat well with his traditional supporters. Bill Heddon, a Moab resident and executive director of the *Grand Canyon Trust*, wrote that "Stiles should be drawn and quartered" for maligning people like Bonderman. When Stiles put out an issue of the *Zephyr* that parodied the "adventure-tour industry" ("There will be a day," he predicted, "when people will only watch a sunrise on tour") and criticized the publication of guidebooks aimed at bringing hordes of inexperienced hikers to once-isolated wilderness areas ("Guide Books Make Good Kindling!"), even his regular readers took offense.

"I am writing," (said one in a letter to the *Zephyr*) "to address that great silent majority of *Zephyr* readers who not only grow desperately weary of your people-hating preservationist hokum, but who indeed thirst for the very information you so selfishly ridicule." Another wrote simply, "We don't need traitors at a time like this." SUWA's executive director, Scott Groene, responded to Stiles by talking to other publications instead of the *Zephyr*. To the *Salt Lake Tribune*: "He's the desert country's own Barney Fife—he's worth having around, even if we have to clean up after him now and again." In *High Country News*: "The environmental movement has not advocated for this new economy. We have raised concerns about guidebooks. We have raised concerns about agencies creating user areas that will only draw more use. But the new economy is being driven by forces that are far greater than we are."

Stiles seems mystified at the enviros' reaction to his tough questioning. "I do not understand how asking the same kinds of questions I would ask of the mining or development industries . . . is wrong." He says he just wants to get a discussion going, even if everyone disagrees. After all, he notes, he got along just fine with the Old Westerners he used to criticize. Mark Steen, the son of Charlie Steen, the uranium king who kicked off the mining boom in the '50s, even wrote a three-part series about his father's exploits for the *Zephyr*. "I learned," Stiles says in the documentary *Brave New West*, "that I could be friends with people whose politics I absolutely abhorred." Over the years, he learned that there are many cattle ranchers who are trying to be "good stewards of the land," that not all Old Westerners are the bad guys, and, certainly, that not all New Westerners are good guys. "When we talk about changing the rural west," he told me, "we're threatening the traditional lives of some very nice people."

You cannot cling hopelessly to the past, of course, without acknowledging its cast of characters. And the issues of the *Zephyr* that have proven exceptionally popular over the years are in fact those featuring old-timers and their stories. Before his death a decade ago, Herb Ringer was a regular in the *Zephyr*. His old photographs of the area and journal entries describing the West in the first half of the twentieth century were immensely popular. Ringer lived alone in a small trailer outside Moab, but Stiles befriended him. "He was like a surrogate dad to me," he says in the film *Brave New West*. The two shared a love of solitude and open spaces. Echoes of Abbey, once again.

"To me, the paper is one-half trying to remember the way things were and then one-half complaining about how outrageous things have become," explains Stiles.

By 2005 the situation in Moab had became outrageous enough to Stiles that he moved to Monticello, fifty miles away. He continued to publish the *Zephyr* in its print form until March 2009.

"This news will come as a sad shock to some of you and a relief to others," Stiles wrote to his readers. "But after 20 years, trying to keep this paper in print is just about impossible." He explained that his decision to speak openly about the "amenities economy" that was destroying the West "put me at odds with my own friends and the very advertisers who keep this paper alive. . . . Seldom do the new owners [of businesses in Moab] want to continue the *Zephyr* ads, and I cannot blame them. . . . I only recently learned a new acronym—ROI. A newly acquired business stopped ads after 14 years and explained it to me. It means 'Return on Investment.' And I can see their point."

And with that, Stiles announced he was taking the *Zephyr* online as the "Planet Earth Edition." "What's happening in Moab is happening everywhere across America and on the other side of the world," he wrote before adding, "The challenge for me is to build an online readership that allows the *Zephyr* to continue as an intelligent, even-handed, sometimes sentimental, frequently annoying, and often irreverent source of information, humor, history and personal reflection on these strange and scary early years of the 21st Century."

When I visited Stiles again at his Monticello home last summer, he was optimistic about the digital *Zephyr*. Twenty-five advertisers had stuck with him right out of the gate, the ones who "don't give a damn about R.O.-fucking-I." He figures he needs 40 advertisers to sign on for about 59 dollars a year to support the effort; that fee represents about a 50 percent reduction from the print version. He also needs about one hundred paying subscribers and that, too, was looking promising.

For someone who claims to be hopelessly clinging to the past, he expresses an amazing enthusiasm for this modern technology. "Online is liberating!" he says. With no printing or distribution expenses, his costs now total 800 dollars an issue, compared to 4,000 dollars for the print edition. He has more content now—15 additional pages in the digital version—and "I can do all color now!"

In some ways, the *Zephyr* lives up to its name perhaps even more in the ether of the Internet. When he was naming the paper, Stiles says in the documentary *Brave New West*, "I thought Zephyr was a beautiful word" meaning "a warm, western breeze." He added, "Of course, it could also suggest I am full of hot air."

A refreshing breath of hot air. Or, as Bruce Anderson would say, "fanning the flames of discontent." Small wonder that Stiles and Anderson use similar metaphors, considering how much these two curmudgeons have in common—an abhorrence of hypocrisy, a determination (bordering on compulsion) to speak truth to power, a passion for a beautiful place, and (cuddly alert!) a love of the folks who live there.

Well, some of the folks, anyway. The rest can go to hell.

CHAPTER FOUR

Too Close for Comfort

Not every small-town editor is cut out to be a crusader or curmudgeon, and only a few have to deal with firebombs or bullets. But almost all of them have to confront the threat of social isolation, of being shunned by their friends and neighbors. Maybe that's why so many of the small-town weeklies are mom-and-pop operations; when the town turns against you, at least you have each other.

A sense of humor also helps. More than one editor I spoke to asked if I knew about the fictitious editor of the *Lake Wobegon Herald-Star*, Harold Starr, whose first principle of journalism is "I have to live here, too, you know." Garrison Keillor, host of the radio show *Prairie Home Companion* and Starr's creator, knows a thing or two about small-town goings-on, about the pressures inherent in the job of being the bearer of bad news. Or even good news, for that matter. And clearly one of those pressures is that when you annoy the people you are writing about, they know where to find you.

This problem is so common that it has long been a regular topic of discussion among small-town editors when they can wrest some precious time away from their jobs to compare notes. I came across a brochure for a conference held thirty years ago in Alaska entitled "Too Close For Comfort: Reporting in a Small Town." The publisher of the weekly *Tundra Drums* in Bethel, Alaska, summed up the essential question for those attending this way: "How do you handle the personal attack? You can't go around busting everyone in the face. And you can't completely dismiss them, because they live next to you or they deliver your oil."

In Bethel, Alaska, the threat of not getting your oil delivered can be serious stuff when the snow hits the fan. Alex DeMarban, who writes for the *Tundra Drums* today, says not much has changed over the years. DeMarban moved to Alaska from Austin, Texas, hoping for some adventure. Working on a crab boat in twenty-five-foot seas provided more adventure than his stomach could handle, so he turned back to journalism, only to find that it could be fairly stomach turning as well.

Alex now travels from village to village by bush plane and boat to cover his rural beat, but he has lived in both Bethel and Dutch Harbor. "It's difficult and emotionally stressful," he tells me, "to have people refuse to talk to you in a small town." One editorial he wrote opposing a pay raise for city employees in Dutch Harbor provoked strong reactions from a lot of locals because the city is one of the largest employers in town. "From this reporter's perspective," he says, "these employees already had a good deal" in terms of pay and "perks," including one airline ticket out of town each year. "At that time, a ticket just to Anchorage cost 850 dollars," he recalls, so he thought it was outrageous that they were seeking a pay raise when so many others in town were barely getting by. And he said so.

"I remember standing in line at the grocery store," he says, "and there was a city employee next to me and he wouldn't talk to me." In a town with just 2,000 permanent residents, that sort of shunning was stressful. "It would have been more bearable if I had been married, had a family. But I was alone. After a couple of cold winters, I got cabin fever and left."

Social ostracism is always chilling, whether you are reporting in the Alaskan tundra or the Utahan desert. Bill Boyle is the editor of the *San Juan Record* in Monticello, Utah, a predominantly Mormon community about fifty miles from Moab. Boyle grew up there and has deep ties to the community and the Church of Latter-day Saints. But that was not enough to inoculate him against the occasional cold shoulder. His first "shunning" came not long after he bought the paper in 1995. "I lost one of my dearest friends," he tells me, "because he was mad about my story on his father-in-law, a county commissioner who was convicted of running a white-collar Ponzi scheme."

Boyle still seems pained by his friend's reaction after all these years. "I believe that was the best work I have ever done. I was very sensitive to the local ties to the community. We ran a feature about the family's long service to the area." The news story about the conviction, however, ran on the front page, and the mere fact of it was enough to trigger the split with his friend and some others in town. "They don't necessarily disagree with how you wrote the story," adds Boyle, "and sometimes they don't even read it. It's the fact that you *wrote* it!"

Boyle is no Jim Stiles, although they are friends and live in the same town. Boyle thinks of himself as a businessman first and a journalist second. After attending Brigham Young University as an undergrad and getting his MBA at Stanford, Boyle became a banker in Seattle. Then, one day while stuck in traffic during rush hour, he had an epiphany. "A funeral procession was holding up traffic, and I realized I was angry about that. Rather than feeling compassion for that family, I saw it as a traffic problem. I realized I had no sense of community. And I wanted to come home, to live simply."

So he came back to Monticello and bought the *San Juan Record*—a popular newspaper that had been published every week for more than ninety years. He knew that he'd never get rich and that the challenge was enormous: "I cover a county the size of Rhode Island, and sometimes I feel like I have a news hole the size of my thumb." This statement implicitly acknowledges that he does, at least, have plenty of advertisers. But he has a small staff of writers that includes his brother, who generously covers local sports for a token twenty-five dollars per week. Boyle doesn't go looking for controversy, and he tries to approach stories with more sensitivity than sensationalism. "I know these people, I love these people. There's heart and soul in local journalism. Big city journalism is nuts and bolts. I prefer heart and soul."

That heart and soul would get sorely tested when an unexpected—and unexpectedly big—story hit his county in June 2009. Dozens of armed federal agents swept into the nearby town of Blanding, Utah, and arrested seventeen people there as part of a two-year sting operation aimed at the black market in American Indian artifacts stolen from public and Indian lands. A total of twenty-four people were arrested in the case, and the majority came from the Blanding area. One of them was a high school teacher (and the county sheriff's brother). Another was the town physician who had delivered most of the babies there, including Bill Boyle.

The day after the arrests, that physician—sixty-year-old James Redd—was found dead in his car. His death was ruled suicide by carbon monoxide poisoning. His wife, Jeanne Redd, had also been arrested and—along with her daughter—would later plead guilty to the charges against them.

Bill Boyle had six days to report this story—one that had new developments each day—and had to handle all the copy himself. It was a very trying experience. "I wanted to accurately reflect the feelings of the local people, but with some eloquence and fairness," he told me in his office on the day the coverage went to press. The front page carried three straightforward stories detailing the federal charges, the federal government press conference in Salt Lake City, and Redd's suicide, which carried the headline, "Prominent Local Physician Takes Life."

> The shock of the June 10 federal raids turned to horror on June 11 when Dr. James Redd, one of the defendants, was found dead near a pond on his property, the victim of an apparent suicide. . . . A large number of area residents fear that the intimidation tactics used during the arrest and arraignment of the Redds may have contributed to the suicide. . . . According to a family spokesman, Dr. Redd and his wife were subject to verbal abuse, threats and taunts before being handcuffed and put into leg irons. They were then put into separate metal cages for transportation to Moab.

Local outrage, says Boyle, centered on the way the arrests were carried out more than the allegations themselves. "Raiding Indian burial sites," he says, "is universally condemned, but there is anger about the way this was handled." Complicating the situation were the differences between the populations in Blanding and his town of Monticello, just twenty-two miles down the road. While both communities have large Mormon populations, the Blanding folks are "extremely paranoid about government interference" and buy into a lot of the right-wing talk in the blogosphere about President Obama wanting to take away their guns and their rights. "The Internet," concludes Boyle, "has unleashed a feeling that 'hateful' is not off limits anymore."

The fact that the raids were carried out by some 150 agents armed with assault weapons and wearing bulletproof vests went a long way to fuel local anger about "overkill." Even those who supported the federal push to stop the looting of artifacts thought the government's raid went too far. Blanding native and archaeologist Winston Hurst, for one, told the *Los Angeles Times*, "The whole point they wished to make is gone. It's completely swamped by the ridiculous imagery of people in their flak jackets taking some old sucker, shackled hands and feet, and shuffling him into the slammer."

Blanding has its own local paper, the *Blue Mountain Panorama* (also known by its critics as the *Blue Mountain Paranoia*), which covered the story "more as a rant" against the government, says Boyle. The *Panorama* editor "may have more accurately reflected the local feelings, but my coverage, I hope, is deeper and broader."

But "deeper and broader" is very tough to achieve when you live in the same town as your sources. Monticello differs from Blanding because it is home to several government offices, including the Bureau of Land Management, the U.S. Forest Service, and the FBI. Because Boyle knows the local residents who work in those offices, he had some insight that the mainstream media covering the story did not have at the outset. He knew that local federal employees had been told to go home on the day of the raids and not participate in them, which they felt was a terrible strategy. One of them told Boyle how angry he was at the way the federal agents made the arrests, but he would not let Boyle quote him by name.

Here's where that "too close for comfort" stuff comes in. What do you do with "inside" information when you are also on the "inside"? "There was no way," says Boyle, "that I could betray his trust. Our kids are friends. We go skiing together."

But Boyle did convince his friend to cough up one quote, which he attributed to "a local federal employee who expressed frustration with the entire process": "'We work for years trying to build a relationship of trust with local residents and officials. Then Big Wigs come down, stir up a hornet's nest and leave for another 20 years. We can only pick up the pieces.'"

Adding to the volatile local reaction was the fact that the feds used an undercover informant in the sting. The informant, acting as an antiquities dealer, secretly recorded his transactions with the defendants and spent more than $300,000 in federal funds to buy more than 250 ancient Indian artifacts. Boyle has no sympathy for those defendants who clearly were excavating sites for rare artifacts, but he wonders if some minor players were victims of entrapment. "Some of these people were doing terrible things stealing from public land," says Boyle. "But dignified seventy-eight-year-old Harold Lyman was not one of them." Lyman, whose family founded Blanding, was in financial difficulty, says Boyle, because his wife had been ill with cancer. "So if someone comes along and waves a lot of money around for artifacts he already owned . . . ?"

In fact, many of the families in the Blanding area have artifact collections that rival those of museums. That's because "pothunting" has been part of the local culture for decades, and some locals still have a sense of entitlement when they find artifacts while hiking the canyons and mesas of this region, which contains thousands of archaeological sites dating back thousands of years. If people find those artifacts on private land, it is legal to keep them. But if they find them on public or Indian land, they are supposed to notify government archaeologists, who can examine the site in a methodical way that preserves the historic information.

Most people, says Boyle, understand the difference between picking up an arrowhead in the back pasture and digging up an Anasazi pot on public land. Dr. Redd, he suggests, should have known better, since he and his wife had been arrested in the '80s for a similar crime. But the authorities failed to win any convictions in that round of arrests, which may have emboldened some people to believe they could still dig and sell with little risk.

Boyle managed to tell the whole story with "eloquence and fairness" by using the words of others, always a handy way to deflect some of the backlash. In the "Letters to the Editor" section, longtime resident and respected archaeologist Winston Hurst made a compelling case for obeying the law when it comes to preserving history. And this was no abstract argument but an intensely personal one.

Dear Editor:

Jim Redd was my personal friend from the time we were toddlers until the end, and when he was available, he was always my doctor. He cared for my aging parents, he delivered my child, he doctored me through injuries and sickness, always with competence and that signature good humor. We shared a passion for things ancient that took us in different directions starting in the 1970s, when he was a young med student and intern interacting with wealthy doctor-collectors, while I was in the army reading archaeology and in graduate school studying it. But our friendship always trumped our disagreements, even when his lust to possess collided with my hunger to study and preserve. This is a huge tragedy, and something deep down inside me wishes that our places were reversed, a wish no doubt shared at this moment by many of our neighbors.

But after all is said and done and the recriminations and anger have settled, we will be right back where we started, faced with the same hard questions (government be damned—this is about us, our personal decisions and their consequences):

Are we a better people if we teach our children to respect the law even when they disagree with it, or should we teach them to hold it in contempt and only obey the laws they agree with?

Are kids better served by being taught to gut and dismantle what's left of our battered archaeological record, or to understand why it's protected, to be respectful and protective of it, and to try to learn from it?

It's always satisfying to rant about big government and to retch in reaction to the whining of self-righteous "environmentalists" (whatever they are) and archaeologists like me, but how many of us in our heart of hearts, if we had the power to decide (oh yeah—we do have that power), would choose to dismantle all protective regulations and open this land up to uncontrolled assault by anyone to do anything they please to it?

Out of respect for Jim, let's not use him as an excuse for behaving like Neanderthals.

Winston Hurst

Juxtaposed to Hurst's letter is an ad for Blue Mountain Gunworks advertising a "RIGHT WING EXTREMISM SALE" for all firearms through the Fourth of July. Even the ads in the *San Juan*

Record provide a window into the emotions of the community, emotions that are not always as nuanced as those of Winston Hurst. And I am reminded, again, that Boyle sees himself as a businessman first, journalist second.

And then there are those times when he is torn between the two.

Even though the funeral for Dr. Redd took place shortly before Boyle had to go to press, he decided not to cover it. "Dr. Redd delivered my children, operated on my wife, but I wasn't surprised when he was arrested," Boyle says in a quiet voice, adding, "He has been intrigued by antiquities for decades." Because of his personal connection to Redd, Boyle admits, he did not want to attend the funeral as a journalist, but since he *is* a journalist, he did not feel comfortable going as a mourner.

And in that one sentence, I realized, he had summed up the lonely limbo of the small-town editor.

"Anyway," he smiled, "that was my deadline day and I had too much to do. And a Blanding funeral is known to last as long as the person's life you're mourning."

As for Redd's obituary, which ran on the back page of the *Record*, Boyle dodged another "too close for comfort" moment by leaving its authorship to the family. If you had not read the rest of the paper, and only knew about Dr. James Redd from this three-column tribute, you might have thought he was pretty much ready for sainthood. We learn that he performed countless surgeries to alleviate suffering, delivered well in excess of two thousand babies (some in cars), made house calls at all hours of the night, and "was a true friend to people of the Navajo Nation and the Ute Mountain Ute Tribe, learning enough of their languages that he could share their friendship and treat their medical needs appropriately."

The cause of death goes unmentioned, along with his hobby of collecting sacred artifacts that, in many cases, came from the lands of the native people he had befriended and served.

The *San Juan Record* is an excellent illustration of how to take a controversial story, cut it up into manageable chunks, and lay it out like a patchwork quilt. In order to get the whole picture, you really have to read it all. Outsiders, says Boyle, think "public opinion in a small town like this is a monolith, as though 100 percent of the people here are wearing straw hats and looking for their pitchforks." While the Red State–Blue State issues are huge, he notes, there are also nuanced shades of purple. He tries to reflect community opinion even as he informs the community of the facts. Problem is, the facts are not always popular. "There will be those who don't think I am covering this story fairly," he says, adding with a grin, "Welcome to Bill Boyle's world."

Boyle's world is not an isolated one, even though he works in relative isolation. It is a world familiar to thousands of small-town editors who grapple with the "I have to live here, too" dilemma. Just down the road, in fact, in Moab, the Taylor family has been dealing with it for a very long time.

The *Moab Times-Independent* has been published since 1896. The Taylor family bought it in 1911, and it is still a mom-and-pop-and-four-grown-children operation. You might think that the editors of a somewhat conservative paper in a town where Jim Stiles's *Zephyr* took so much of the heat might have ducked the "too close for comfort" dilemma. But when I sat down with sixty-eight-year-old Adrien Taylor in the *Independent*'s office in Moab, she answered my question about that issue by posing one of her own: "Have you heard of Harold Starr?"

Even though she identifies with the fictional editor's slogan of

"I have to live here, too," she adds that "we are not the chamber of commerce newspaper and we have never held back" out of concern for what friends might think. That means, of course, that friends sometimes get mad. "I just keep my head up, put a smile on, and go on down the street."

They made one of their strongest editorial stands against a move to put a nuclear waste depository in a canyon near Canyonlands National Monument. At the time, the area was suffering an economic downturn before the tourism boom. "This town almost came to blows over this one," she remembers, with some people adamantly opposed because of the environmental danger and others in favor because of the economic benefits. "I was afraid we would have a shooting" before it was over. "This paper," she says proudly, "said NO" even though there was a strong chance of losing some advertisers. "We have always made it clear that advertising and news are two different things. If you don't like the news and you are an advertiser, tough shit."

Spoken like someone who has experienced quite a bit of pushback over the years. "Even small stories can turn into firestorms in a small town," she says. And sometimes the reasons are not immediately clear. Adrien says they recently reported a story about the local hospital volunteering to do a CT scan on an ancient artifact, a bundle owned by the Canyonlands Historical Association. Because the wrapping was so fragile, they felt it would be safer to use technology to see what was inside. "We did the story," says Adrien, "and then two days later, we got an irate call from one of the doctors. He railed on and on about what a horrible piece of journalism it was and how we'd gotten the story wrong." After further probing, she discovered the only thing "wrong" with the story was that "we hadn't mentioned his name."

Knowing when to name people, in other words, is just as touchy a subject as knowing when not to name them. Small-town editors tiptoe through this minefield every single week. But if there were an award for Tactful Tip Toeing, the *Dove Creek Press* would have to be a contender.

Dove Creek is a tiny Colorado town just across the Utah state line. I would never have bothered to visit this newspaper or the somewhat eccentric couple that owns it had it not been for the serendipity of picking up a copy on my way through town one day. Half the front page consisted of a photo above the caption, "Totaled." The photo showed a wrecked car overturned on someone's front lawn. The headline (a "glass half-full" approach if there ever was one) read, "Only One Seriously Injured in Accident." This lead paragraph followed (and no, I am not leaving anything out):

> The amazing part for Colorado State Patrol Trooper Joe Wilson was that no one else was injured during the accident last Sunday afternoon. "There were many eye witnesses and children on bikes when the accident occurred," he said, "I am impressed no one else was hurt." The accident left passenger Kelsi Cobeen, 17, of Durango, with severe back injuries and in the hospital in Grand Junction.
>
> The accident occurred at around 1:00 pm. The driver, Dennis "DJ" Ford, 20, of Dove Creek, had turned off Highway 491 and was coming down Fourth Street, after getting lunch at the Superette. Exactly what happened next was clear to Officer Wilson, but why it happened is still unclear.

This back-door approach to a front-page story may have been poorly written by almost every traditional standard, but I couldn't stop reading. It was the journalistic equivalent of slowing down to gawk at a car wreck, which—in this case—had the advantage of being more than a metaphor. I was rewarded with one of the "best" examples of burying a lead I've ever found.

The reader learns next that the car driven by the local lad ("D. J.") had swerved off the road, snapped a power pole in half, rolled two times, and landed near the base of a tree. His passenger (Kelsi, the girl from out of town) was ejected from the car and thrown twenty feet into the air. She landed on the roof of a nearby house and then fell to the ground.

This is the last we hear about Kelsi, by the way, until the end of the article, which continues on another page. The story focuses mostly on D. J., who is, after all, from Dove Creek. It approaches delicately the question of just how he managed to crash in such a stupendous way.

"What caused DJ to lose control of the vehicle has not been determined. He reportedly has a seizure disorder caused by a brain tumor, but doctors had assured the family that he probably would not have a seizure while driving. Stress does increase his chances of a seizure, however, and it had been a stressful day for DJ. He accidentally ran over his dog earlier that morning."

Call this the "for want of a nail, the shoe was lost" style of storytelling. By the time we get to the end, the impact has diminished somewhat. A more traditional approach would have been to lead with the fact that a young man known to be prone to seizures had been allowed to get behind the wheel of a car, resulting in an accident that would likely leave his passenger paralyzed for life. But I get ahead of myself (or, at least, ahead of this version of the story).

D. J., we learn, suffered a few bruises but no broken bones. As for his passenger (who may or may not have known her driving companion had a brain tumor), we finally learn that "her

most serious injury is crushed vertebras five through eight,"
and that she is scheduled for surgery to graft a new vertebra
from her hipbone.

"The doctors have said there is a 99% chance she will not
walk again, but the family reports that Kelsi is looking to the
1% chance she still has."

The *Dove Creek Press* clearly likes to accentuate the positive.
In fact, it is something of an unwritten policy of the married
couple that owns it.

When Doug and Linda Funk bought the newspaper in 1983,
the previous owner, Mike Bonan, had some words of advice: "A
small town editor can serve to pull the community together or
tear it apart. You have to make your decision right now about
the kind of editors you'll be."

Ironically, while both Funks agreed they wanted to be the kind
of editors who united the community, they themselves seem to
disagree about almost everything. "I want to be more critical
of public officials," says Linda. For example, when Dove Creek
school board members announced, after the fact, that they had
taken a trip to Mesquite, Nevada, for a school board conference,
Linda wanted to investigate further. After all, the members took
their spouses, like it was a vacation. And there was gambling
there! But Doug was, as always, the good cop to her bad cop,
and the two of them finally decided not to ask any embarrassing
questions. After all, they told me, they knew the board members
personally and knew their "moral character," and they did not
think they were capable of squandering taxpayer dollars on a
wild time in Mesquite. So, no questions and no story.

But weren't you abdicating your watchdog role, I ask them,
by avoiding the issue? With that, Linda glares at Doug and says,
"Answer THAT, Mr. Funk!"

And he does. "If we found a political official misusing tax-payer funds," he responds, "we wouldn't hesitate to nail him to a stump." By way of example, he points to a story they did about improvements, including a new ditch and fence, to a county road that happened to be next to the property of a county commissioner's relative. It was "gotcha" journalism, Dove Creek–style.

"When we get cross-wise with elected officials," adds Linda, "we look 'em in the eye and say, 'next election we'll help you out.' As in, out of office."

I sat down with the Funks in what can only be described as a funky office. Their office supply–printing business sits up front (many small papers bolster their income this way), while an old printing press is in the back. Their very old dog Jasper (credited as the "newshound" in their masthead) lies at their feet. Neither of them makes any claim to having known anything about journalism when they took over the newspaper, but they have come to love the job. Their lives, in fact, are consumed by their dedication to covering everything that happens in Dove Creek and the surrounding communities. The paper is much more than a business venture. "We handle the *Dove Creek Press* with loving care," says Linda. For better or worse, this commitment sets them apart at social events. "I'm looking forward to the day when I'm invited to an event," says Linda, "and they don't say 'bring a camera.'"

Doug got his college degree in animal science and came back to Dove Creek to work his mother's farm. "That's when I realized," he says, "that I actually hated cows—catching them, branding them, the whole thing." He then tried working at the High Country Elevator (a bean and wheat facility) and he hated that as well. So when the Dove Creek Press came on the market, the Funks bought it for thirty thousand dollars—"lock, stock, and barrel."

"Our biggest problem," they confess, "is making a living at this." The paper's health depends on the relative prosperity of the region. When a uranium mine closed in 1984, the region lost two hundred jobs. Stores closed and ad revenue dropped. But things are looking up, say the Funks. A new uranium mine may be opening up (though not everyone in the area sees this as a positive development), and a new biodiesel plant recently opened in Dove Creek, which relies on locally grown sunflowers to provide the raw material for energy. The groundbreaking was a huge event for this little town of 700. More than 300 people (and the governor of Colorado) showed up for the festivities.

"Sunflowers will be the savior of this area," Doug proclaims, in a fairly typical example of Funk optimism. "I understand how hard it is to be a farmer," he says, but he believes sunflowers could be more lucrative as fuel and food than the traditional crops of wheat and pinto beans. And besides, adds Doug, who jogs by the sunflower fields every day, "it's hard to be sad with that view in front of you." When the sunflowers are in bloom, they provide a nice alternative to the usual photographic fare of the *Dove Creek Press* front page: half-page shots of various farm implements in a field. In fact, tractors are so ubiquitous in these pictures that the paper sometimes looks like a trade publication. But tractors in a field are, in their way, calming in their sameness. And the Funks are not interested in stirring things up unnecessarily. They most certainly are not interested in making things worse.

Take, for example, the story they did NOT print about how little league players from the upscale resort town of Telluride always found an excuse to avoid traveling to Dove Creek for games. The Funks learned that a father of one of the Telluride players was a certain rock star who was "afraid he would be mobbed" in Dove Creek. The implication was that Telluride was used to celebrities, whereas the hick town of Dove Creek would be agog at having such a famous person arrive in their town. The Funks had heard that this man was willing to pay each Dove Creek family fifty dollars for the cost of bringing their Little Leaguers to Telluride for the game. The insufferable arrogance!

The Funks would not tell me the name of this "rock star," so I had no way to verify the story. But they did explain to me why they decided not to dig into the story further or print it. Because of Dove Creekers' hostility toward the hoi polloi of Telluride, they say, "printing that story would only make things worse."

The editor of the *Telluride Watch*, Marta Tarbell, may cover more "high-end" issues, but she is subject to the same "low-end" pressures. She and her husband Seth Cagin were journalists in New York City before buying the *Watch*, where they soon learned that "everything you do has a 'backatcha' quality," Tarbell says. "This has changed the way I think about journalism. Now I take a 'defense attorney' approach rather than a prosecutorial approach. You have to tell these stories fairly." That means, she continues, that she sometimes breaks "a cardinal rule of journalism" and allows people to see their quotes ahead of time, to make sure she has quoted them accurately. "I've never regretted it," she adds.

There are many kinds of stories that local editors choose to handle with kid gloves. For the Funks, one of them is sexual assault. "Everyone in town knows who it is," they point out, "so why write the name and all the upsetting details." And Linda, who usually handles the more difficult stories, is proud of the fact that she never uses the word *suicide*. In the case of a sixteen-year-old boy who committed suicide, she says, "I said he died of a self-inflicted gunshot wound to the head." That might not seem like a big difference to an outside reader, she says, "but it mattered to the family."

Because of the difference in their personalities, tough-minded Linda handles the phone calls inquiring into deaths and accidents, while good-natured Doug handles the occasional angry phone calls from readers who may take issue with an article. Certainly Doug is the more emotional of the two, which is why, says Linda, she handles the more emotionally charged interviews. In fact, Doug choked up a couple of times during my visit—once when he was describing his brother's difficult life as a farmer, and once when he was talking about how his dog, Jasper, was beginning to fade. "When I have to take him out to shoot him one day," he said with tears in his eyes, "I'm going to bring two bullets." Linda had no comment.

Truth be told (and they do manage to do that, even if you have to decode their "bury-the-lead" style), the Funks are an endearing yin-and-yang editorial couple that is sincerely dedicated to serving the community. "We see our role as a helping profession," says Linda. Referring to the typical etching on a gravestone indicating the length of a life, Linda remarks, "You do more than get born and die. It's what you do in 'the dash' that counts."

As for their tendency to bury the lead because, hey, they have to live there, too, they are not alone. One story from my town paper, the *Norwood Post*, provides another example. It began by saying that a number of residents had come to a meeting of the town trustees to protest what they saw as the overzealous actions of the new deputy sheriff, who had pulled over a number of residents for breathalyzer tests late at night. Only toward the end of the article do we get a clue that the protest was somewhat biased. The reporter wrote, "Before adjourning, the mayor said that, in the future, he would not tolerate drunkenness at a public meeting."

The drunks had showed up drunk to protest being pulled over for driving drunk. Now, that's a lead. But anyone who wanted to ferret it out had to read to the end of the piece.

Once you get the hang of it, decoding the small-town paper style becomes somewhat addictive. I am often rewarded with new finds simply by sampling papers in towns I am passing through, like the *Dolores (CO) Star*, "The Voice of the Dolores River Valley since 1897." Under the headline "Lux Resigns as Dolores Mayor," we read a letter by Mayor Tommy Lux: "Due to recent circumstances with my personal life and town issues, I feel that my positive overall attitude will be affected and my best judgment, for which I was elected, will now be impaired." In further remarks made to the paper, Lux says that had he stayed as mayor, "I wouldn't have been laughing and outgoing and fun. I would have been a different person, and that's not right." And, finally, this: "My resignation had nothing to do with Ronda . . . or any people in town."

Nowhere in the article do we learn the identity of this Ronda person, although we are pretty sure that she did, in fact, have something to do with it. This is small-town journalism code for "if you have to ask, you don't live here, and if you don't live here, we don't care what you think." But if you do live there, and you happen to be the editor of the paper, you do care what people think. Up to a point, anyway.

That point is often the intersection where telling the truth collides with a friendship or financial pressures. Jim Kevlin, editor of the *Freeman's Journal* in Cooperstown, New York, says "you can put a price tag on an editorial decision." Writing in the *American Journalism Review*, Kevlin recalls that when one potential advertiser wanted access to news columns, "that was a $2,000 decision to say no." But that is the price you pay, he concludes, for "the joy of weekly newspapering." Al Cross, the director of the Institute for Rural Journalism and Community Issues, says the small-town editor is "always one or two advertisers away from bankruptcy."

The decisions made in that crucible provide a test of integrity and courage week after week. And a surprisingly large number manage to pass it, despite the financial pressures. At that "Too Close For Comfort" conference in Alaska three decades ago, editor Ted Hall put it this way: "It's the toughest reporting, but it's the chance to do the best reporting because you're writing the great human novel bit by bit."

Or, as the Funks would put it, it's what you do with the "dash."

1. Laurie Ezzell Brown in a rare moment of relaxation
at the *Canadian Record* in Canadian, Texas, 2009.
Courtesy of Cathy Ricketts.

2. Bruce Anderson, editor of the *Anderson Valley Advertiser*, at home in Boonville, California, 2004. Courtesy of Mark Scaramella.

3. George Ledbetter, editor of the *Chadron Record,*
in Chadron, Nebraska, 2010, delivering the paper.
Courtesy of Kerri Rempp of the *Chadron Record.*

4. Tom Gish, editor of the *Mountain Eagle*, in
Whitesburg, Kentucky, 1967, with his printing
press. Courtesy of Tom Bethell.

5. Jim Stiles, editor of the *Canyon Country Zephyr*, in his home office, 2006. Courtesy of Mark Fox.

6. Jason Miller, editor of the *Concrete Herald*, in Concrete, Washington, 2009, on Main Street. By the author.

7. Twin Rivers Detention Center, Hardin, Montana, the focus of a contentious local story, 2008. Courtesy of Michael Dillin, former editor, *Big Horn County News*.

8. M. E. Sprengelmeyer, in the office of the
Guadalupe County Communicator, on his first day as
publisher — August 1, 2009. Sprengelmeyer bought
the weekly newspaper in Santa Rosa, New Mexico,
after the *Rocky Mountain News,* where he had been
the Washington correspondent, closed its doors in
February 2009. Photo by Mark Holm © 2009.

CHAPTER FIVE

This Town Isn't Big Enough for the Two of Us

Few people had heard of Hardin, Montana, (population 3,600) before the spring of 2009. That's when the town made national news by offering up its new and never occupied Two Rivers Detention Facility for the purpose of housing Guantanamo detainees.

Almost every news organization in the country—and some from outside it—covered the story. The narrative was always the same: a plucky Western town, hit by hard times, was willing to take prisoners no one else wanted for both profit and patriotism. As one resident told *Time* magazine, the dry, wintry plains of Montana "would be torture for some of those boys." Another pointed out that it would be tough for people of Middle Eastern descent to escape and blend into Montana's homogenous population.

The story came to a fairly abrupt conclusion after the Montana governor and both senators (Democrats, all) aggressively rejected the idea. "I understand the need to create jobs, but we're not going to bring Al-Queda to Big Sky Country," said Senator Max Baucus. "No way, not on my watch."

By now, of course, most Americans have forgotten the whole thing. It was one of those amusing little stories that surface for a news-cycle nanosecond, sporting headlines like "The Montana Town That Wanted to Be Gitmo," and garnering the requisite fifteen minutes of fame on the *Today* show.

But in fact, the story of the empty prison was always more interesting and complex than those cutesy headlines and clichéd scripts implied. I stumbled on the story a year before it made the national news, back when it consumed local press attention for very different reasons. And I only happened upon it because I had been looking for a town that supported newspapers with competing agendas. Hardin, I discovered, was an ideal test case. And it had the added benefit of being next to a place I had always wanted to see, the Little Bighorn Battlefield National Monument.

Little did I realize that I would be stepping onto a new battle-field that mirrored the original in many ways.

When Lieutenant Colonel George Armstrong Custer led his Seventh Cavalry into the valley of the Little Bighorn River, he was not terribly well informed. He was clueless, for example, about the location and size of the enemy, a rather big "oops" in military intelligence terms. More than a century after the Sioux and Cheyenne wiped out Custer and his men in the rolling grasslands of eastern Montana, the truth is still an elusive com-modity in these parts. Not only is the battle itself still a subject of contention (the National Park Service did not add an Indian memorial at the site or include the Indian version of events until the 1990s) but so is almost every interaction between the Native Americans and the rest of the population currently liv-ing here. Racism (on both sides) is rampant, racism nourishes distrust, and distrust breeds conspiracy theories. "What they really want is to drive us out so they can have the land" is the most common narrative (on both sides), and narratives breed newspapers.

Three, to be exact, in a twenty-five square mile area: the *Big Horn County News*, the *Apsáalooke Nation*, and the *Original Briefs*.

"If you're in a war zone, there will always be news," says Wes Eben, the publisher of the *Big Horn County News* in the town of Hardin. "And there is a constant war between the [Crow] tribe and everyone else." Eben has mixed feelings about Crows' seemingly hostile attitude. "This tribe would not exist, would have been annihilated, if it weren't for the white man. The Cheyenne and Sioux tried to wipe out the Crow and the Crow were down to below a thousand people when the military intervened. Of course," he hastens to add, "there's distrust on both sides. And rightly so. The kids are brought up on it. Both sides have done things to each other over the years."

"That's putting it mildly," says Scott Russell, tribal secretary and publisher of the Crow Agency newspaper, the *Apsáalooke Nation*, when I asked him about this legacy of distrust. "My mother grew up here when there were signs in Hardin that said 'No Dogs and No Indians Allowed.' We'd like to see things change, but racism is alive in Bighorn County."

Eben says part of the problem is that ever since Hardin was carved out of reservation land back in 1907, the townspeople have felt as though they are "living on the edge of a third-world country." In addition to the joblessness and poverty, Eben tells me, "we see . . . Native Americans drinking on the corner, panhandling on the street, passed out in the alleys."

"I'll be the first to admit," Russell states, "that we have that harsh reality here. There are people who want to look at us as a third-world country. And we might be."

Does that offend him?

"As a tribal member, yes, but as a tribal official I might be able to use that to get more money for our people. You look at the federal government giving billions of dollars to rebuild Iraq. They could spend some money on Indian Country."

That's the sort of attitude that galls Eben, who says most Americans do not really understand reservation life. "They see the unemployment and poverty," he says, "which are real. What they don't see is that sadly a lot of that is the result of the welfare state, the welfare thinking." Even so, he hastens to add, the tribe has some legitimate grievances about the past. "The White has done a lot to injure the Crow over the years."

And certainly journalism has done its part, right from the beginning. The first account of the Custer defeat appeared in the Dakota Territory's *Bismarck Tribune* on July 6th, 1876, and it pretty much set the tone for decades to come. "MASSACRED" screamed the headline, followed by the subheading: "No Officer or Man of Five Companies Left to Tell the Tale." The word *massacre*, of course, connotes wholesale slaughter, rather than a valiant battle between warriors. In other words, the ones who tell the story get to shape the "truth." Buried at the bottom of the article ("aged" replicas are sold as souvenirs at the Custer Café across from the battle site) is an afterthought: "We said of those who went into battle with Custer none are living. One Crow scout hid himself in the field and witnessed and survived the battle. His story is plausible [sic] and is accepted, but we have not room for it now."

No room for it? In that one paragraph, we find more "truth" than the writer ever intended. Even though Crows served as scouts for Custer and were also enemies of Cheyennes and Sioux, the fact that this particular Crow scout (known as Curly) was the only survivor did not elevate him to the rank of "sole survivor" in the reporting of the story. There was no man "left to tell the tale"—that is the headline. Here was a living eyewitness whose account was considered plausible (which is, apparently, a feather shy of credible), and the paper chose to leave it out. He was, in other words, a nonperson whose voice was not deemed worthy of hearing.

When I first decided to write about the competing newspapers in this sparsely populated area of eastern Montana, I was suffering from some major misconceptions of my own. I had already spoken on the phone with the publishers of the *Big Horn County News* in Hardin and the *Apsáalooke Nation* at the adjacent Crow Agency, and the story, as they say, was writing itself—always a dangerous proposition. The headline forming in my mind was along the lines of "Plucky Indian Tribe Starts Own Paper," with the subhead, "100-Year-Old White Paper Won't Tell Their Stories."

As it turns out, I was about as well informed as Custer when it came to the complexities of the situation on the ground. Nothing, absolutely nothing, about this situation fit my preconceived notions. I arrived in the community of Hardin, about two hours east of Billings, as preparations were getting underway for the annual June reenactment of the Battle of the Little Big Horn. Two reenactments, actually. Every year at the same time, the community of Hardin and the Crow Tribe stage competing reenactments of the Custer battle. These battles, which basically follow the same script (with the same obvious ending), take place within miles of each other. The tribe's reenactment is the highlight of Crow Native Days, an event started in the 1990s.

"All the tourists," says tribal secretary Russell, "used to drive right past Crow [Agency], and Hardin would make all this money." The Native Days celebration, he says, was aimed at luring some of those dollars away, and also at keeping the Crow people away from Hardin. "We have a dry reservation, alcohol is illegal," he explains. "Back in those days, the kids were going to Hardin, getting drunk at the street dances, getting into fights, getting into car wrecks."

But they knew they needed a special hook to attract the tourists. A Crow brochure advertising Native Days, available in Hardin motels and restaurants, tells visitors that "The Battle of the Little Big Horn takes place daily on Friday, Saturday and Sunday at the Real Bird Ranch located right at the historic Medicine Tail Coulee where the battle actually took place."

The Hardin reenactment occurs some distance from the actual battlefield. Even so, both events are well attended, probably because both the Crow Agency and the town offer other festivities and competitions—from the tribe's "ultimate warrior challenge" (canoeing, running, and horse racing) to Hardin's annual Bed Race down Main Street (two people push, one rides).

Given the historical backdrop of animosity, Wes Eben gives a remarkably evenhanded account of the various competitions in the *Big Horn County News*. He intersperses updates on the Custer battle among reports on all the races and competitions. He wrote in one piece, "If there was an Iron Woman award this year [for the Crow Tribe's "Ultimate Lady Challenge"] it should go to Grace Bulltail. Due to one of her team members not showing up she did both the running and canoeing for her team. Back in Hardin the Little Big Horn Days Parade was getting under way. This year's theme was Past, Present and Future. Little Big Horn State Bank's float depicting a large bag of gold, a dollar bill and a debit card won first place."

The juxtaposition of these two culturally disparate events—one celebrating athletic prowess, the other financial prowess—is not intended as an editorial comment.

Eben can't resist, however, poking fun at the plethora of reenactments, a sort of "Groundhog Day" for Custer's ghost. "Friday at 1 p.m. Custer lost again both in Hardin and at Medicine Trail Coulee." Then, several paragraphs down, "It is now 1 p.m. on Saturday and, yes, Custer loses again . . . twice in Hardin and once again at Medicine Trail Coulee." And, finally, "Custer and the 7th Cavalry lost two more times on Sunday."

But the real competition is not about the "casualties." It's about the cash. The article quotes the Hardin Chamber of Commerce as saying that it sold twelve hundred tickets for each of its four Custer's Last Stand reenactments, adding, "no count was available at press time on the number of attendees at the Real Bird re-enactment."

This article, by the way, is headlined, "Doing Battle Then and Now." There is, I am sure, no irony intended.

To fully appreciate the undercurrents that keep three newspapers afloat in such a small area, a cast of characters comes in handy. It would certainly have come in handy for me, but as I had no scouts riding ahead, I had to discover these characters and their connections myself. In the interest of simplifying a rather twisted yarn, I offer the following guide to the newspapers and their staffs when I visited them:

THE PAPERS
Big Horn County News

Founded 1908. A weekly based in Hardin, Montana, published by the Yellowstone News Group, circulation 2,000.

Owner: John Sullivan. A hands-on manager, especially when advertisers call to complain.

Publisher: Wes Eben. A ruggedly handsome man sporting a cowboy hat and a beleaguered expression. Retired Navy pilot and high school guidance counselor, two jobs that just barely prepared him for his current combat position.

Editor: Michael Dillin. A veteran print and TV journalist from Jacksonville, Florida, who saw an ad for the editor position and thought it would be nice to wrap up his career with a quiet job in a beautiful place where he "could write stories about little old ladies planting gardens," a classic example of Custer-think.

Reporter: Jim Eshleman. Does not always take kindly to having his copy edited, an interesting stance for someone who admits "I suck as a writer." Also pens a column called "Simply Biased," which makes it easy for readers to know where he stands (to the far, far right).

Apsáalooke Nation

Official newspaper of the Crow Tribe, located at tribal headquarters in Crow Agency (Baaxuwuaashe), Montana. Published weekly. Circulation 2,000.

Publisher: Scott Russell, of the Bird In Ground family. Also serves as tribal secretary, an elected position that gives him the responsibility of communicating tribal news and, at the same time, makes the journalistic task of "questioning authority" much easier.

Editor: Ben Cloud. Says his last journalism training was working on the high school paper, but he is learning fast. Proud of circulation figures (2,000) and the competitive pressure the tribal paper has created in the area for both news and advertising.

The *Original Briefs*

Established in 1975, a daily "rag sheet" (as the competition calls it) that looks like it was printed in someone's garage on 8 1/2 x 11 inch paper folded in half. Has a small picture of underwear on the masthead. May look amateurish (spelling errors abound), but gets grabbed up immediately in local motels and restaurants. Competitors deride it as the "*National Enquirer* of Hardin," full of gossip and unsubstantiated rumor. And lots of ads. Claims 7,000 circulation, a number dismissed by the competition ("some people pick up seven at a time"). Printed daily.

Chief News Writer: Joe Fitzpatrick. Describes himself as a white man married to a Crow woman, which means "I am trusted to an extent in both places and, to an extent, not trusted in both places." Believes the area would be a lot better off if both sides would just "drop their cultures."

I soon discovered the perfect prism for viewing the intense competition and longstanding grievances of all these players in Big Horn County: the saga of that jail built by the city of Hardin in 2007 for twenty-seven million dollars. Funded by revenue bonds and turned over to a for-profit management agency, the Two Rivers Detention Facility was envisioned as Hardin's largest economic development project in decades: it would create over a hundred jobs and house more than four hundred prisoners.

Only there were no prisoners. Seems the town officials had great faith in consultants who assured them, essentially, that "if you build it, they will come." They didn't.

Enter Mike Dillin, the newly hired editor of the *Big Horn County News*. He arrived in Hardin in February 2008 from Florida looking forward to writing his share of folksy features. Instead, he walked into the kind of battle that has historically ended badly for outsiders in these parts. As he puts it, he took one look at the flap over this empty jail and thought, like any sensible reporter would, "'Holy CRAP! You guys built this thing without a contract to put prisoners here?' It's like building a major league baseball park without a team!"

Dillin was telling me all this in his distinctive southern drawl over hamburgers on the day I arrived in Hardin, several days before he would be fired. But I get ahead of myself. That morning, after downing my free "continental breakfast" of miniature bagels and corn flakes at the local motel and watching copies of the *Original Brief* fly off the counter (and making a mental note to look into that phenomenon), I picked up a copy of the *Big Horn County News* and read an account of recent developments in the prison story headlined "Crow Tribe Blocks BIA Involvement with Detention Center." Dillin and Jim Eshleman shared the byline, which would prove to be critical.

Hours after officials of the Hardin Detention Center won a court battle to allow out-of-state inmates to be housed at the facility, the project plunged deeper into controversy when Crow Chairman Carl Venne made good on his word to block the center from getting a contract with tribes from the National Congress of American Indians (NCAI).

"I am writing to express the Crow Tribe's vehement opposition," Venne said in a letter to the chairman of the NCAI, Joe Garcia. "The Crow Tribe attempted to assist (Hardin), . . . but they went on record stating that they were "not interested in any solution that involves the Crow Tribe."

Venne called it "infuriating" that Hardin officials went to other tribes "located thousands of miles away, in order to solve (Hardin's) growing problems."

Venne closed his letter by saying the Crow Tribe "opposes any other tribe or Indian community in aiding the City of

Hardin in connection with the Two Rivers (Hardin) Detention Facility."

On May 15, in an exclusive interview with the *Big Horn County News*, Crow Chairman Venne said he had been insulted by Hardin officials when he began working to have the facility taken over by the Bureau of Indian Affairs (BIA).

"You'd think they'd be happy to have a $27 million problem taken off their hands," Venne said in the interview. He added he would not only refuse to support the facility, but would use his power make sure other tribes did not utilize it either.

"There has been a huge miscommunication between the city and tribe," said Hardin City Attorney Becky Convery. "We'll take a certain amount of blame for that. What needs to be done, is to repair the situation and be open to communication."

Hardin officials say the facility would create 100 jobs, and 70% have been promised to those of Native American origin. Big Horn County has the fourth highest unemployment rate in the state.

(Publisher Wes Eben contributed to this report).

Since I had no background on this story, I had to read the article (longer than I have included here) a couple of times to digest the basics, which boils down to this: the town had built a twenty-seven million dollar prison by floating revenue bonds, was unable to get a contract to house prisoners from the county or anywhere else in the state, and then tried to find a way to import prisoners from outside Montana. The Montana attorney general issued a legal opinion saying that Hardin could not import prisoners under state law, a ruling Hardin appealed and won. At the same time, Hardin was trying to work out a deal with the Bureau of Indian Affairs and the National Congress of American Indians to help import some prisoners when the chairman of the nearby Crow tribe, angry that the town had sidestepped him, managed to block any agreement. Now the town was again stuck with a twenty-seven million dollar white elephant (emphasis on white) and facing foreclosure.

Hell of a story, I thought, and nicely written. It packed in a lot of information and colorful quotes, covered both sides of the issue, included the latest developments, and supplied the reader with the backstory.

That's what was on my mind, anyway, as I drove up to the office of the *Big Horn County News* at the end of the main street, tucked between the old Hotel Becker and the Custer General Store, just across from the railroad depot. The coal trains run almost continuously here, representing one of the few consistent sources of revenue for the Crow Tribe. (They lost the land the coal mines are on but not the mineral rights.) I had the newspaper in my hand when I walked through the door and met publisher Wes Eben and his wife, Barb, who works the front desk. When I was introduced to the editor, Mike Dillin, I said, "You're the one who wrote this story? Nice job. I really enjoyed reading it."

The room went silent. Dillin turned a bit red and said, "Thank you. I really needed to hear that today." I had clearly made some sort of gaffe but could not imagine what it might be. Sitting in Eben's office, door closed behind us, I found out that this article had unleashed holy hell. According to Eben, newspaper owner John Sullivan was aware that town officials were threatening to pull their legal advertising, and Sullivan believed Dillin had shown bias in this story from the beginning.

Come again? I reread the article, but could not see the problem. Eben agreed that this particular story was well written, but he said there was a contentious history that contributed to the eruption over this seemingly balanced report. And it had to do with the man I had just complimented—the editor from back East, Mike Dillin, the stranger who lived by a different code.

"Mike came in with what I call the Tin Man reporter concept: you are protected, you don't associate with the people you report on, you have no relationship with them, nor do you have a desire to have one," Eben explains. That worked for Dillin in his capacity as a big-city reporter, he continues, but not in Dillin. "He had no concept of small town reporting. You can still tell the story, but you write it in a way that makes it clear you are part of the community."

Over lunch a few hours later, Dillin defends his approach. "Wes encouraged me to join the Kiwanis Club, like the last editor, but I don't do that. I was trained not to do that, but to keep an objective distance." He adds that his work in Hardin "is as good as any work I've done in my life and that includes interviewing two presidents."

Apparently this was something Dillin had mentioned more than once. "I don't give a rat's ass if he interviewed a president," volunteers reporter Jim Eshleman when I finally caught up with him. "I told Wes I could not work in the same office with that man. I know I suck as a writer, that I didn't come up to his standards, but he expected me to worship him and I didn't."

As if the confrontation between whites and Crow Indians was not enough to keep things lively, now there was a culture clash on the *Big Horn County News* staff. Not only was Dillin an outsider who refused to get chummy with the townspeople, he was also horrified by the town's overt racism against the Crows. "It's worse than anything I ever saw in the South," he tells me, an observation that does not sit well with the locals. "People accused me of being 'touched by a feather'"—the modern version of "Injun-lover."

Eshleman, however, is the fourth generation of a local Hardin family. He remembers "the time ten Crow kids ganged up on a white kid" when he was in high school in the 1970s, which led to fighting and rioting in Hardin. He was surprised that I had never heard of the "Hardin riots," an event that apparently ranks in his mind right up there with the Battle of the Little Big Horn. At any rate, he says, these sorts of incidents over the years have left an impression, but he insists that it is based on fact, not racism. After all, he reports, "Whites and Cheyenne get along well." (The enmity between Cheyennes and Crows predates Custer.) Eshleman also says he works hard to keep his opinions out of his reporting. "I would never change quotes in a story [something he accused Dillin of doing], although I might make the quote grammerically [sic] correct."

In other words, the two men were polar opposites and on a predictable collision course. Eshleman, on the one hand, leans far to the political right, using his "Simply Biased" column to ridicule, among other things, the notion that humans had contributed to global warming or to sympathize with ranchers who employed the "shoot, shovel, and shut up" approach in dealing with federally protected species like the wolf. At the same time, he dislikes swear words, peppering his own emotional statements with "Criminy!"

Dillin, on the other hand, is no stranger to expletives picked up from working in various newsrooms over the years, and his language offended Eshleman. Even worse in the eyes of Dillin's enemies, he had once worked as a volunteer for Barack Obama. This was before he came to Montana, he says, at a time when he was not a working journalist. Still, the connection would come back to haunt him when his job at the *Big Horn County News* was on the line. Obama's campaign appearance on the

Crow Reservation in May 2008 was the first by a presidential nominee since the '60s, and it received heavy coverage in the tribal paper. But it was the extensive coverage in the *Big Horn County News* that outraged some Hardin residents.

Such outrage is puzzling unless you have been immersed in the distrust and paranoia of Custer-land. While any journalist would take such an event as big news in a small community and consider it certainly worthy of in-depth coverage, the Hardin city attorney believed Dillin had a sinister motive. In fact, Rebecca Convery told me she believed Dillin had taken the editor's job in Hardin so he could work as a "stealth" campaign organizer for Obama. "He was down there (the Crow Reservation) when Obama got 'adopted' by the tribe! My GOD," she said, "he wrote TWO stories!"

One of those stories was headlined "Obama 'Black Eagle' Soars in Big Horn County" and reads, at least to the nonparanoid observer, as a straightforward account of a highly unusual event.

> Likely Democratic presidential nominee Barack Obama made history Monday, making a rare 100-mile roundtrip by bus in the midst of a crowded campaign schedule to visit the Crow Indian Reservation in Big Horn County. A crowd of approximately 2200 people—mostly Native Americans—poured into the veterans park to hear the Illinois senator pledge to honor treaty obligations, provide help to Indian health services and to name a permanent American Indian advisor to his White House staff.

To City Attorney Convery, this kind of coverage over time showed a clear bias on Dillin's part. "It became blatantly obvious," she told me, "that he is pro-tribe, pro-governor [Democrat Brian Schweitzer], pro-Obama, and anything that WE might say otherwise will not get out."

I interviewed Convery at her office, which was located in the otherwise deserted Twin Rivers Detention Center on the edge of town. When I walked up to the gate on the outer fence of the barbed-wired perimeter typical of many prisons, I waited for some sort of sentry to buzz me in. The sign in front of me warned, "NOTICE: NO HOSTAGES WILL EXIT THROUGH THIS GATE." As I waited, I had a lot of time to think about what that meant, exactly. Was it a warning that guards would *shoot* hostages before they would allow prisoners to use them as shields in an escape attempt? Or did it mean that hostages would, in fact, exit through *another* gate? The sign's obtuseness seemed appropriate, somehow, to the setting. Finally, a voice called out, "Just push the gate, it's open!" It was a strange sensation, walking into a prison with no prisoners. It almost looked like a movie set, something they might want to contemplate if things don't turn around.

My meeting with Rebecca Convery was yet another ambush on my preconceived notions. I had expected the city attorney of Hardin to be a hard-boiled Republican with deep roots in the community. Not so. Convery had moved to Montana from the East Coast with her gay partner. She is a Democrat. She says she was not prepared (her own Custer moment!) for a political landscape split down racial lines. Whites are a minority and the Crow hold a majority of elected positions in the county, including (at the time) sheriff and two of the three county commissioners.

"I'm a Democrat, but this [the prison project] has changed some of my fundamental beliefs," she says. "What I have seen is when you are a non-Indian and you live in a border town and you live in Native American majority districts, really the shoe is on the other foot. Suddenly the non-Indians have no voice in their county government, in the state government, in the federal government. The state politicians are beholden to the Indian vote and the tribes know that."

Convery and the other Hardin officials believe that the Crow chairman, Carl Venne, had negotiated with Governor Schweitzer and the Bureau of Indian Affairs behind their backs in an effort to take control of the prison and, by extension, the land it sits on. Her suspicions were fueled by a visit from the tribal attorney. "She wanted to know our alternatives if we lost that lawsuit filed by the Montana attorney general" to keep Hardin from importing prisoners from out of state.

This question, apparently, was Convery's "aha" moment.

"Now we figured that this lawsuit was a delaying tactic" by the Crow in cahoots with the state, one "aimed at dragging things out until we defaulted on the bonds." She adds that "the investors would have no choice but to sell this thing. And who's the likely purchaser?"

A dramatic pause.

"We believed," Convery continues, "that the Crow tribe was trying to acquire the facility in a federal takeover which implied that the property would then become reservation land." If that happened, she says with a meaningful look, "There will be incidents."

Reenactments, anyone?

The Crow have denied they are engaged in a plot to take over the prison, and one longtime observer of tribal culture, Denny McAuliffe, thinks it is a far-fetched idea. McAuliffe, a professor at the University of Montana, is a former *Washington Post* reporter and has served as director of reznet.com, a site that mentors young Native American journalists. "Whites come up with conspiracy theories," he says, because there is a complicated effort underway by the federal government to help Native Americans buy back some of the land they have lost over the years through something called "fractionated heirship." This has to do with an old Crow tradition of not drawing up wills before death. "When grandma dies," says McAuliffe, "she does not have a will, so all the relatives inherit. Eventually, a one-acre plot can have a thousand owners, which is a block to economic development."

The federal government, as part of a recent lawsuit settlement with Native Americans, has established a two billion dollar fund to buy up fractional interests in land. The idea is to consolidate ownership for the tribes so that they can reap the financial benefits of the natural resources on those lands.

Wes Eben and other Hardin-ites think it is outrageous that the taxpayers should help the Crow consolidate their real estate, saying it would come at the "expense of the livelihood of the ranchers in the area." Eben says the Crow could withhold tracts of land now leased by the white ranchers for grazing their cattle.

McAuliffe believes such conspiracy theories are unfounded: "The Crow aren't that well organized." And he also disputes the notion that the governor and senators are hostage to the Indian vote. "It's only with Obama's visit here that Indian voter registration has gone up." And that happened well after the prison controversy was under way.

But paranoia has deep roots here, as firmly imbedded as the prairie grass waving over the Little Bighorn battlefield. And so the prison has become the modern symbol of all those years of suspicions and slights. In Convery's words, "We view this as the poster child for expansion of the reservation boundaries."

And into this landscape of hidden ambushes rode Mike Dillin, the wordslinger from out of town, whose first story on the subject was a legislative hearing in the capital of Helena. His headline: "Hardin: 'You've Got a Problem.'"

Helena—A state panel today questioned how the City of Hardin could build a $27 million dollar detention facility with no promises from the state or federal government to house inmates there.

"Our purpose is not to rehash history today, but to say we have a $27 million dollar facility and beds that can be used to detain inmates and treat them for drug and alcohol problems," said Rebecca Convery, the city attorney for Hardin.

"I cannot answer why (we) did not have contracts in place," Convery said. "But I can say we had reputable bond counsel."

But advisory council members repeatedly returned to the issue of how and why Hardin moved forward with such a big project while having no secure revenue stream to pay for it.

A member of the advisory council, Channis Whiteman of Crow Nations, said he had been hopeful that the Hardin facility would be a success because of the jobs it would provide.

"But you should have had a bulls eye on the target before going forward with this project," Whiteman said.

Montana Lt. Governor John Bohlinger sounded an empathetic note. "We're not going to resolve this problem at this hearing," Bohlinger said. "But we're concerned about all of the citizens in Montana, because when any of Montana's communities have a problem, then all of Montana has a problem.

"The City of Hardin has a problem."

They had a problem, all right, Convery tells me. The problem was Mike Dillin and his "slant" on this story. "We looked at the article and said, 'Were we even at the same meeting?'" From her point of view, Dillin did not report all the testimony that supported their investment in the facility, including their allegation that state officials had "led them to believe" there would be a need for more prisoner beds in Montana. In addition, the town commissioned three separate studies that showed there would be such a demand.

Any reporter who has ever covered a controversial subject has heard similar complaints. When the complainers say, "You're not telling both sides of the story," what they really mean is, "Our side is right, and your reporting didn't make that clear." In a big city, such complaints—if unfounded—can be shrugged off. But in a small town, a town wallowing in decades of "us versus them," it can have some serious blowback.

"Michael Dillin has slaughtered us," Convery tells me.

There's that word again.

Dillin rode into town in February and was gone (at least from the job) by July. In those months, his articles were a growing irritation to Convery and Hardin officials, who thought the reporter was missing the obvious: that Governor Schweitzer was purposely ignoring them and working with the Crow. "The governor would repeatedly visit the Crow tribe, twelve miles up the road," Convery explains, "and he was repeatedly invited to come up here and meet with city officials and he refused to do so. That went on for two years."

And so, in March 2008, dozens of disgruntled residents of Hardin boarded buses for the state capitol to get the governor's attention on the prison issue. Dillin's front-page headline struck a note of boosterism:

TOUCHDOWN HARDIN: Governor Pledges to Visit Detention Center.

Helena—Almost 200 Hardin residents descended upon the state capitol building Tuesday, looking for something between a hand-out and a showdown. What they got was a promise that Governor Brian Schweitzer will finally travel to Hardin and tour the controversial $27 million dollar detention center with 464 beds and no inmates.

Straightforward enough, it would seem. But—apart from the headline—apparently the article did not have ENOUGH booster-ism for the newspaper's management. In an ominous sign for Dillin, the same issue carried a front-page story praising staff reporter and columnist Jim Eshleman.

ESHLEMAN COLUMN GETS STATEWIDE ATTENTION

We don't mean to be "simply biased."

But our man, *Big Horn County News* columnist Jim Eshle-man, has been not only the talk of the town, but the talk of the state after lampooning Montana Governor Brian Schweitzer over the issue of Hardin's empty detention center.

Jim has made it clear that he blames the governor for the $27 million jail being empty. That's because the state has refused to put prisoners in it. Jim called the governor a "bully." And that's before Jim became more critical.

Jim even coined a new term for the community's treatment by Helena—"you've been 'schweitzered.'"

Mike Dillin did not heed these warning shots. Instead, he dug in his heels, convinced he held the higher ground. "I am a reporter, I am a journalist," he tells me, and "to push away from a story is too hard." His dogged determination might have won more plaudits had it been in service of the more popular version of the "truth" in Hardin: that the state was conspiring with the Crow Indians. For people in the community, Jim Eshleman was that "truth teller." Dillin was not "one of them."

And that chasm widened to epic proportions when the governor made good on his promise to visit the detention center on April 1. Convery was outraged that the governor gave no advance warning to Hardin officials. Instead, he showed up at the town's detention facility with the Crow tribal council. "Our reading was that they [the governor and the Crow chairman] were standing against the city of Hardin." If there was a turning point in this battle, it came here. Even Mike Dillin had to concede that his reporting veered into analysis and commentary when he wrote about the governor's visit.

> Governor Brian Schweitzer made good on his word—and more—by coming to Hardin and touring its empty $27 million dollar detention center and to hear the city's plea for help to make it a success.
>
> "I will do everything in my power to make sure this facility does not default," Schweitzer told nearly a hundred citizens who had showed up to witness his much anticipated tour. "We're going to have to do the best we can with a horrible situation."
>
> But for any of the governor's critics who thought he might have in some way been contrite, apologetic or even on the defensive, they instead saw a state chief executive who was clearly in charge and in control. And if it was a political game being played out, Schweitzer played it as if Hardin was his home turf.

This flattering description of the governor would have been bad enough for Dillin's readership, but what came next was sure to inflame them.

> City attorney Rebecca Convery began describing the familiar tale that state officials had all but urged Hardin to build the facility. Schweitzer lit into her.

"The trouble with the shifting of positions is that somewhere along the line you decided to say it was my fault," the governor remanded. And he didn't let up. "How is it that the blame has shifted from the people who decided to build this facility, borrowed the money to build this facility and worked with BIA and the federal government, and now you've shifted it to me personally. Honestly, I want to know."

Then he dropped the hammer.

He reached over and pulled out a banner that had been displayed during the so-called March on Helena last month. The banner read: "We've just been Schweitzered. Governor, was it as good for you as it was for us?"

He unloaded.

"I know you brought a lot of high school kids with you (to Helena), so I presumed that (the banner's doing) had to be some of them, but there are also some adults who live in this community. And if those adults are condoning something like this, and shifting the blame from the responsibility of those who made these decisions to a person who wasn't even governor when this began, at some point, before we can move forward in legitimate ways, people have to take responsibility for decisions they make."

The article goes on to describe how the executive director of the detention center, Gregg Smith, apologized for the banner that had been hung in the state capitol. (The fact that the phrase "you've been Schweitzered"—a euphemism if there ever was one—was coined by a writer for the *Big Horn County News* who takes pride in never using the "F" word apparently never came up.) Dillin's report went on:

From that point on, much of the tension eased.

Schweitzer took great note to say that Crow Tribal Chairman Carl Venne had "been doing a lot of heavy lifting" to pursue the possibility of whether the center might be used to house inmates held federally by the Bureau of Indian Affairs. "I look forward to working with Chairman Venne on this matter," Schweitzer said. It seemed an unmistakable signal that the road on which the governor and Hardin leaders must travel is one that goes through the offices of the chairman of the Crow Tribe.

To Convery, this report was proof that Dillin was "100 percent biased." And, she says, she was not alone. "I know at least half a dozen community members who have gone to Wes Eben and complained."

Eben, the publisher, was feeling the pressure from folks in Hardin and, he says, from the paper's owner, John Sullivan, who had been made aware of complaints from some of the bigger advertisers (like the bank that contributed that parade float with the giant debit card). But even as Eben was chastising Dillin for veering into commentary in his report about the governor's visit, he was still hoping that Dillin—a talented editor and writer, in his estimation—would adjust his attitude and be more of a "team player."

"We try to convince the city people that we [the newspaper employees] live and die with the town, too," recalls Eben, but Dillin insisted on casting himself in the role of Objective Outside Observer. It was an attitude, feared Eben, that could have financial ramifications. "The price of ads is determined by your circulation. And your circulation is determined by how pleased people are to read your articles. And if people are ticked at you, they won't be buying your paper."

And people were definitely ticked. "I deal with these hits constantly as I walk the streets," says Eben, "and I deal with my advertisers who pull me over to talk with me. Dealing with mistakes we have made in the writing, that's difficult." Even so, Eben did not fire Dillin. Not then, anyway.

If it had been up to Convery, however, Dillin would have been gone long before the incident she considered the last straw: he landed an "exclusive" interview with Crow Chairman Carl Venne, printed it on the front page, but never called Convery to ask her to respond to the charges made by Venne in that interview. "That's when I stopped talking to Michael altogether," she tells me. "I feel that he won't report it [our side of the story], and if he does, he will spin it."

Not that Convery's voice was totally absent from the article. Venne granted the interview because he was angry about a letter he had received from the city attorney. He shared Convery's letter with Dillin, who printed it:

> I am writing this letter in an attempt to repair the strained relations that have developed between the city of Hardin and the Crow Tribe concerning the Two Rivers Detention Center. The crux of the problem from our perspective is as follows: over the past several months it has become increasingly apparent to city officials that the Crow Tribe has a desire to purchase the facility upon default of bonds and take land back into trust for the Tribe. To be blunt, that is not a solution that the City of Hardin or the Two Rivers Authority is interested in.

As Venne concluded, "If that was an attempt to reconcile, it sure doesn't sound like it."

Venne told Dillin he was insulted by Convery's suggestion that Crows were conspiring to take over the prison. The town, he said, had earlier asked for his assistance in working with the BIA to bring in prisoners.

> I was talking with the Bureau of Indian Affairs, and was trying to see if I could help get them to use the Hardin detention center, instead of building a new multi-million dollar facility out at Fort Peck. You'd think Hardin officials and taxpayers would be relieved if [the federal government] could have opened that place. I was trying to take people off the hook. But now, I really don't care. They slapped me on the cheek once and I'm not going to turn my cheek and let them slap it again. They (Hardin officials) have made it clear they don't want us (Crow Tribe) around. Well, that's fine. We don't need them anyway.

It probably would have been an excellent idea for Dillin to call Convery for her reaction to this inflammatory interview. While it is not hard to imagine what her response might have been given her previous position and the sentiments in her letter to Venne, calling for a reaction is Journalism 101.

And speaking of Journalism 101, the fledgling tribal newspaper *Apsáalooke Nation* was also covering the detention center story, but in its own unique style, which has nothing to do with any of the principles taught in journalism schools. The governor's visit to the detention center, for example, was headlined enthusiastically, "Governor in Hardin!" The article provided a "Rashomon"-like glimpse into the story, one told from an entirely different perspective. Reading between the lines (which I have taken the liberty of doing) is half the fun.

> The governor of Montana along with Chairman Venne made the effort [we're doing you a favor, Hardin] to visit the Hardin

detention center amid concerns of defaulting on its financial obligations [they really screwed up!]. The Hardin facility is still empty and still has no contracts [not that we're rubbing it in]. Governor Schweitzer says he is willing to help the center with anything to make sure that it will eventually open. He was also disturbed by the blaming that has been forwarded to his position. [The peculiar sentence structure is part of the fun in deciphering this paper]. When the center was being built Governor Schweitzer said he was not even in office so he questioned why the community shifted its blame on him. [Those townspeople blame everyone but themselves!] Since the center is located in Big Horn County, and has the highest unemployment rate in the state [that would be us], Chairman Venne took an active role with Governor Schweitzer in recent times to seek possible solutions to help the Center with housing prisoners from the federal side, which seems a good possibility that could take place with the chairman's influence at the national level. [Show some respect, Hardin, our guy has clout!] In recent interviews Hardin officials seemed angered and felt bullied [we know how that feels!] by this position that the Chairman has taken with the Governor. Now it seems there is mistrust of both Venne and Schweitzer that the Two Rivers Authority will be left out, which is clearly not the case. [We offer no evidence, but this is the official tribal newspaper, so just take our word for it.] During the tour Venne said, "We are willing to work with you on possible solutions, and I believe we can work together." [We own the high ground.]

As I said before, I came to this area thinking I would be writing about a plucky Native American newspaper that started out because the white paper in town was not telling "their" stories. Turns out that was true. It just wasn't the whole truth.

As you drive the twelve miles of interstate from Hardin to Crow Agency, there is no doubt you are entering Indian Country. The exit sign spells "Crow" in the native language, "Baaxuwuaashe," but other "signs" spell poverty: dilapidated trailer homes, abandoned store fronts, muddy potholes. I drove past the reservation campus of Little Big Horn College and a statue inscribed with the words of Chief Many Coups: "Without education, we are the white man's victim." It seems everything is viewed from a counterpoint position, which is hardly surprising, given the history and grating juxtaposition of these two worlds. The office of Scott Russell, tribal secretary and publisher of the *Apsáalooke Nation*, is located in an old hospital that has seen (at least one hopes) better days.

Russell is a tall, imposing man who is treated with deference by his staff. He is, I realize, very much like his counterpart in Hardin, Wes Eben; both come across as natural leaders who are used to handling conflict with a certain amount of aplomb. Russell started *Apsáalooke Nation* a few years ago as the official voice of the Crow Tribe. "As tribal secretary," he tells me, "one of my duties is to communicate what is going on in tribal government." But he also wanted to create a kind of "good news" alternative to the *Big Horn County News*. "Every time you pick up the *BHC News*," says Russell, "there was something negative about the tribe." He cites the detention center story as an example. "If you look at that, it's a one-sided story. We tried to help them [Hardin officials] at the beginning and they got threatened by it. They thought that we wanted to take over their jail." Now, he chuckles, Rebecca Convery is saying it is all a "misunderstanding" because she is running for election and Crows are a big voting bloc.

I had to concede that this is not a point of view likely to

be published in the *Big Horn County News*. And yet BHC *News* publisher Eben says he was often frustrated in his attempts to get news about the tribe in his paper. "The Crow were sending us press releases they called 'news stories,'" Eben remembers, "and they would say 'we want this printed as a news story.' And I would say, 'That's an advertisement for the Crow government position. If you want a news story, we will interview you about this and it will not all go in the paper.' And they didn't want that."

No argument there, says Russell, with no apologies. He started *Apsáalooke Nation* to promote the Crow culture and language. "Before, rumors would fly and—because tribal politics are vicious—rumors would bring people down. Now we can disseminate information."

"So," I ask gingerly, "they trust that you are telling the truth?"

"They should!" he answers, adding, "In my line of work you have to expect that some won't believe it."

"There's no Letters to the Editor section?"

"Do you think I should put one in there?"

"I do," I venture.

He thought about it for, oh, three seconds.

"No, the letters would just be negative, and we want to promote the positive aspects of our culture."

When I relate this conversation to Dennis McAuliffe, of reznet. com, he laughs. Scott Russell is a friend of his, but he has no illusions about Russell's role as a "newspaperman." "What you are going to get" with most Indian papers, McAuliffe says, "is government statements. Are they good papers by our standards? No. You cannot be a journalist there. If you are worth your salt as a reporter you will be fired from a tribal paper."

Last year, Russell took his small newspaper staff to Missoula to meet with McAuliffe. "I wanted Denny to attack our paper big time, I wanted our staff to see it from the point of view of a profession." And did he? "Yes," answers Russell, laughing, "he told them if you have been fired from a tribal paper then you are doing good because you are doing your job!" Russell tells this story with no sense of hypocrisy. He wanted the staff to hear a professional critique, but he had no intention of changing the way he does things.

Russell's editor, Ben Cloud, is not quite as rigid about these issues. Cloud spoke to me on a hilltop not far from the Little Big Horn River, where tribal members were preparing for the annual Sun Dance. He wore a bandana around his forehead and a welcoming smile, and he spoke openly about the tough line he walks in putting out a paper in which the tribal elders have the final say. Unlike Russell, he sees a more independent future for the *Apsáalooke Nation*.

"The tribal administration sees the potential of the paper as a business, and I think soon we could go on our own and be independent from the tribal government," says Cloud, adding that if that happens he would like to see tribal law amended to contain a "freedom of the press" provision.

McAuliffe has never seen that happen. He points to the case of Bonnie Red Elk, from Fort Peck Indian Reservation in Montana. She was fired from the reservation paper because she was "committing" real journalism, says McAuliffe. So she started her own paper, the *Fort Peck Journal*, "where she is free to speak the truth." But she faces two challenges according to McAuliffe: "she must stay afloat financially and she has lost sovereignty protection against libel now that they [the paper's staff] are not affiliated with the tribe."

Ben Cloud is optimistic, however, and sees the Crow paper as a force to be reckoned with in the area. "Prior to this tribal newspaper, you seldom saw Crow news in the *Big Horn County News*. Now you see it flooded because I think they are a little threatened by our existence. They feel a little competition now, which is good."

The competition, of course, is in the form of ad sales. But Cloud, who is clearly not on the same wavelength as Russell, wants to compete with content as well. He would like to add "Letters to the Editor" and even a police blotter one day, he says. Right now, the "Crow Tribal Arrest Report" is a regular feature in the *Original Briefs* in Hardin, perhaps because it requires no original writing. And for those just traveling through town, it may provide their only introduction to some of the more colorful Crow names in the region.

Michael Takes Enemy, arrested for Disorderly Conduct.
Alvin Pretty on Top, arrested for Disorderly Conduct.
Gary Yellowmule, arrested for possession of intoxicants.

One unusual last name, White Man Runs Him, dates back to the days when Crows and the U.S. Cavalry were allies.

At any rate, the editors of *Apsáalooke Nation* are satisfied, for now, with its focus on positive tribal spin. It also aims to be an educational tool by printing some parts of the paper in the Crow language, right down to the page numbers: "Page Dúupe, Achievers, Page Dáawiaa, News, Page Sápua, ads."

Ben Cloud would like to write more of a rebuttal "to this popular story over there in Hardin, the prison story. Those people in Hardin thought we were trying to take it over." Then again, if he was privy to the battle waged by journalists in Hardin over that story, he might be content to ride in the other direction and let the townsfolk inflict their own wounds.

Which is just what happened.

Michael "Touched by a Feather" Dillin had ruffled plenty of *other* feathers in his short tenure as editor of the *Big Horn County News*. The week I arrived in town, those feathers were already flying. Here is how it played out:

Wes Eben had left town the week before, to attend his daughter's wedding in California. Just before he left, the town of Hardin won its lawsuit against the state attorney general, giving them the right to go out of state to find prisoners for their still-empty detention center. Shortly after that news broke, Crow Chairman Carl Venne successfully blocked an effort by Hardin to work out a deal with other tribes to bring prisoners to Hardin's facility. So the *Big Horn County News* had major developments to report in its most controversial story. Reporter Jim Eshleman wrote up an article that Wes Eben saw before he left. He told Dillin, the editor and primary writer, that he thought it needed changes.

Eshleman's story read as follows (punctuation and "grammerical" errors are his):

> The Two River Detention Center which was built by the Two Rivers Port Authority, last week won its court battle with the state allowing it to house out of state prisoners. Hardin's Economic Development Director Greg Smith traveled to Reno Nevada to attend the mid-year session of the National Congress of American Indians (NCAI) where a resolution was introduced that would give the Detention Center the support of the NCAI for the contracting of bed space at Two Rivers Detention Center by the BIA.
>
> In a letter to the NCAI, Crow Tribal Chairman Carl Venne expressed the Crow Tribes vehement opposition to the NCAI resolution.
>
> This letter led to the defeat of the resolution.

It goes on in this nearly incomprehensible manner for two more pages. Dillin took one look at this and rewrote the copy. You have already seen much of that story, but for comparison purposes, just take another look at his lead: "Hours after officials of the Hardin Detention Center won a court battle to allow out of state inmates to be housed at the facility, the project plunged deeper into controversy when Crow Chairman Carl Venne made good on his word to block the center from getting a contract with tribes from the National Congress of American Indians."

As writing samples go, this is no contest. Dillin reworked the piece, using pertinent quotes from Eshleman's version but also including more of the history of misunderstanding and enmity between the tribe and the town over the detention facility. He emailed the edited version to Eben, who approved it. "I thought this final version came across as balanced," Eben told me on the day I first visited his office. "I laughed when I saw that he added my name to the bottom so all three of us would get shot at. Then I found out when I got home that it was true; we all *were* getting shot at!"

And some of it was "friendly fire." When Jim Eshleman saw the revised version on Thursday, the day the paper came out, he was furious. "I thought Mike had biased the piece," he explains. He was especially upset that his name was included in the byline (Dillin thought he was doing Eshleman a favor by crediting his reporting on the story) and that he had not been told of the changes.

So Eshleman marched into the newspaper office on that Thursday and demanded an explanation. And this is where things get murky, because the only two people there were Eshleman and Dillin. Eshleman's version: "He went ballistic. Called me a motherfucker. He stood up and charged me." Dillin says he did not threaten Eshleman physically or verbally, but he does not deny that they exchanged angry words. Eben listened to both versions when he returned and concluded, "The two accounts are totally opposite. One of them is a liar."

But before Eben could even return to Hardin from California, before he knew there was a battle underway, Eshleman rode out and summoned reinforcements. First, he went to the police to file an incident report. Wasn't that a bit extreme, I ask? "Criminy," answers Eshleman, "he charged me and I was afraid he was going to hit me!" Then he tracked down Rebecca Convery. "Becky and I talked," he says.

Actually, it was more than talk. Eshleman handed over to Convery his original script of the story so she could compare it to the one that ran in the paper. "She didn't like my version either, but she thought Mike had biased his piece."

Forget for the moment that handing over a confidential work product to an outspoken critic of your editor would be grounds for suspension or dismissal at most news organizations. What Eshleman did was essentially pour gasoline on the fire Convery had been stoking over a period of many months. I compared the two stories written by the two reporters, line by line, and could find no substantive differences in content.

But Convery was not about to let facts get in the way at this point. She immediately phoned John Sullivan, the owner of the *Big Horn County News,* who she believed was already upset by the report Dillin had written earlier on the governor's visit to Hardin (and the resulting backlash from advertisers). Eshleman had delivered the last bit of ammunition she needed to go after Dillin. Convery put it all in a follow-up letter, which she faxed that very day to Sullivan. The letter was headed, "RE: Bias in the Big Horn County News" and is printed here in its entirety:

Dear Mr. Sullivan:

Thank you for taking the time out to speak with me this morning. As I expressed over the phone, I have strong concerns that the City of Hardin is not getting a "fair shake" from the new editor of the *Big Horn County News*, Michael Dillin.

In fact, it seems clear to me that Mr. Dillin's political agenda comes through loud and clear in his reporting concerning the Two Rivers Detention Center in Hardin. Whenever the City of Hardin has been at odds with our democratic governor or with the Crow Tribe, Mr. Dillin has very clearly taken up sides with the Governor and the Tribe.

As you know, however, there are two sides to every story. Up until this morning, reporter Jim Eshleman has provided some balance to Mr. Dillin's venomous opposition to the City of Hardin in the stories he has authored concerning the detention center.

However, this morning a front page article appeared in the *Big Horn County News* entitled "Crow Tribe blocks BIA involvement with Detention Center." The article was originally researched and written by Jim Eshleman and was reviewed by Wes Eben prior to publication.

However, it is my understanding from Mr. Eshleman, that before the article was published, it was rewritten by Michael Dillin without Jim Eshleman's knowledge. The end result, once again, the City of Hardin got the short end of the stick.

So what is Mr. Dillin's motivation? The answer in my mind is quite simple—Mr. Dillin is a campaign organizer for Barack Obama. All one has to do is search for Michael Dillin on the web, to see what his political agenda is—ensure that Barack Obama is the next President of the United States. Accordingly,

Mr. Dillin's bias in favor of the Crow Tribe seems blatantly obvious.

While I applaud Michael Dillin for his political activism, I deplore his very obvious use of the *Big Horn County News* as a mechanism to further his personal political agenda, regardless of the cost to the local community.

If Mr. Dillin wishes to express his political views in the paper, then perhaps he should consider writing an opinion column, as Jim Eshleman does when he wishes to freely express his opinion.

In the meantime, the *Big Horn County News* may risk losing one of its finest, Jim Eshleman, who grew up in this community, and who has served the paper and the community well. I wonder how long Michael Dillin will stick around Hardin after November 3rd, when his work here will be done?

For your review, I have attached copies of the article in question as originally written by Jim Eshleman and as edited by Michael Dillin. The third is a fundraising letter from Michael Dillin that went out days before Michael Dillin reported on his first story on the Hardin Detention Center.

I would ask that you consider retracting Michael Dillin's story and allow Jim Eshleman to publish the story as originally written and researched.

Very truly yours,
Rebecca A. Convery
City Attorney

Dillin posted the fundraising letter she refers to on the Obama campaign's Web site. When I asked him about it, he said he wrote it in February while he was still living in Florida, before he took the job with the BHC *News*. He noted that the date on it—March 8, 2008—was wrong. In any event, it was not a fundraising letter but an invitation to Obama supporters to gather at a hall in Jacksonville for an organizational meeting. In the online memo, Dillin introduces himself by giving his background as a journalist, then says: "This is really the first time I have been free of the constraints of the mainstream media, so I can personally get involved in this campaign."

Wes Eben returned from California to find a stack of urgent messages from John Sullivan. In fact, he was just getting ready to respond to all of them and trying to figure out who had done what to whom when I walked through the door with my cheery compliments for the editor who had written this fine story. Given what I have learned since then, I am amazed that he kept the appointment.

Even as we were discussing these developments in the privacy of Eben's office, another ambush was in the works. It seems that Eshleman had gone to the competition—the *Original Briefs*—with his tale of editorial injustice.

According to *Original Briefs* writer Joe Fitzpatrick, Eshleman came in and once again outlined his grievances over Dillin's editing. Fitzpatrick says it was a question of "journalistic integrity, that's what that flap was all about. Jim's piece was rewritten in a way he didn't approve, but his name was still on it." Fitzpatrick adds that this sort of thing is "the cat's meow" for him, because he likes "investigating and getting to the bottom of things."

Only he did not investigate. I doubt that he even compared the two stories. And he certainly did not bother to consider, if he knew it in the first place, that editors are *supposed* to change reporters' copy. What part of the word *edit*, I wondered, did these folks not understand? At any rate, Fitzpatrick simply took Eshleman's word that this arrogant outsider had massacred his work, and so, under the guise of defending the principles of journalism (and no doubt salivating at the thought of embarrassing the competition), Fitzpatrick printed a story on the front page headlined "B.H.C. News Article Skewed by Writer."

In the article published in the June 12th edition of the Big Horn County News entitled "Crow Tribe Blocks BIA involvement with Detention Center," there are several points that need to be made in order to give a neutral view to the situation and to point a finger at the person who actually edited the original writer's article, apparently, to suit his own agenda.

The Two Rivers Detention Facility is still a hot topic, but fuel doesn't need to be added to the fire by one-sided news articles. Our job as publishers is to report the news and give the opportunity for both sides to be heard to give the readers the opportunity to make their own decisions.

From sources close to *The Original Briefs*, we were given the original article written by Mr. Jim Eshleman. . . . [A]s it was originally written, the article showed both the view points of Chairman Carl Venne and City Attorney Rebecca Convery, but the article that was published in the paper's June 12th edition was not what was written by Eshelman.

Instead the article that was published had been edited by Michael Dillin and the editions that were made skewed the story to a point that did not allow either sides of the controversy an even playing field [*sic*].

When I ask Jim Eshleman about his apparent collusion with the competition, he first denies giving them his article. "I did not go to the *Original Briefs*," he tells me. But when I inform him that the *Briefs* reporter was very clear about the fact that Eshleman had come to the other paper with the information, and that he has no reason to lie to me, he backpedals, saying he just meant to say that he had not *encouraged* them to run the story. "They like to stir it up," he says.

Indeed they do. And indeed they did. By the end of that week, the weight of opposition to Mike Dillin had reached critical mass and he was fired. Eben called him in and told him he "did not fit in here." Dillin believes he was punished for being objective, for refusing to get "too close" to those he was covering.

Not true, says Eben. "It had nothing to do with his writing, he was a very good writer. But he added his own emotions to the [prison] story and that inflamed people. And his aloofness made it worse. One of these people had to go. We are a four-person office and people have to work well together."

Eben was troubled, too, by the date on that Obama Web site memo, which "indicated Mike was still working for them" (the Obama "people") after he took the editor's job. "That put doubts on his veracity." What's more, the owner of the newspaper chain, John Sullivan, wanted Dillin out. "I agreed with him, finally," says Eben, "because the situation had gone on long enough."

Eshleman thought he might lose his job as well for sharing confidential work with outsiders. "Wes put a piece of paper between his fingers and said, 'You came this close to being fired.'" Eben confirmed this telling: "Jim was so pissed [at Dillin] he made an almost fatal error. He gave his copy of the original script to Convery. He should never have done that."

But in the end, the error was *not* "fatal." Eshleman walked away, the sole survivor, with nary a scratch. And unlike the account of Curly, the Crow scout and sole survivor of the Battle of the Little Big Horn, Eshleman's version of events got wide play.

In the official National Park Service handbook of the Little

Bighorn Battlefield National Monument, historian Robert Utley wraps up his description of Custer's demise with a question:

> How could it have happened? The question reverberated up and down the Army chain of command and quickly spilled over into the newspapers and public journals. And it has echoed through history to this day.
>
> The largest current of thought washes up Custer as the culprit. Thirsting for glory, he was accused of disobeying orders, taking a direct instead of a circuitous route to his destination, attacking with an exhausted command and without adequate reconnaissance. . . . A truer explanation is simply that Custer's legendary luck deserted him. Knowing neither terrain nor the exact location or strength of the Indian camp, he had to grope forward half blindly, allowing his battle plan to take shape as circumstances unfolded. By the time he knew enough, it was too late.

Ah, hindsight.

Mike Dillin now knows something about the dangers of taking a direct route into unfamiliar terrain, not to mention the pitfalls of hubris. Even so, he says he would not have done anything differently. He told me he regretted not being able to follow up on a lead about a fifty-thousand dollar payment, possibly linked to the detention center bond money, made to a nearby town's police department. He thought the transaction seemed strange since the town has *no* police department. "I was waiting on the right opportunity to make a public records request. I was being careful, because the heat was on continuously for me not to do stories on the detention center."

The *Big Horn County News* replaced Dillin with an editor from Red Lodge, Montana, named Shelley Beaumont. "There is a peace and calm that has settled over the office," says Eben, "now that Mike is gone." Eshleman tells me he liked her, too. "Mike never introduced himself to people who came into the office, and she does."

What's the difference, I ask?

"Ahhhh," he sighs. "She's a Montanan."

Meanwhile, down the road in Crow Agency, home to people who were Montanans before there was a Montana, *Apsáalooke Nation* continues to publish only positive news about the tribe.

Doing otherwise, after all, could get you fired.

POSTSCRIPT

As of this writing, the Two Rivers Detention Facility remains empty and the twenty-seven million dollars in bonds is in default. There was a brief flurry of excitement when a fellow from California named Michael Hilton arrived in Hardin to say that his company, American Police Force, would not only fill the vacant detention center with prisoners but also provide computers to local schools, start a homeless shelter, and feed the hungry. Not bothering to look too deeply into this rather improbable stroke of good luck, the Two Rivers Authority signed an agreement with Hilton to take over the operation. Alas, it soon emerged that Hilton was a convicted felon with multiple counts of grand theft who had used more than a dozen aliases in various fraud schemes over the years. The American Police Force and its prisoner population were about as real as the musical instruments promised by Professor Harold Hill in *The Music Man*. Only not nearly as amusing.

Other developments: Rebecca Convery resigned as city attorney; tribal chairman Carl Venne passed away; Wes Eben left his position as publisher to work for a local car dealership; Mike

Dillin moved on to other journalism jobs in the West. And the *Big Horn County News* has yet *another* new editor, Brett Thomas-DeJongh, a young man armed with a master's degree in journalism from the University of Montana as well as high hopes for bringing quality reporting to Hardin. "It's a pretty exciting place," he tells me. "It feels like the Wild West. It's a place where you can use what you learned in journalism school. I think people have gotten away with things in the past, politicians in the county. We're a weekly paper and we should be looking into these things." Given the fate of those who have gone before, we wish him luck. This territory claims a lot of casualties.

Actually, one thing has not changed: the *Big Horn County News* continues to publish Jim Eshleman's column. In a recent rant about the future of the prison, he wrote, "Let's face facts: our governor and the DOC [Department of Corrections] apparently have no plans to use this facility as it was intended. In fact, they seem to be going out of their way to make sure it's not used. Unless, maybe, if it's sold to the Crow Tribe?"

Oh, and Custer and his men continue to die each June.

Several times, in fact, and in different places.

CHAPTER SIX

All the Names Unfit to Print

Let's face it: the police blotter is the best stuff in the paper, the place we turn to first, the place where we learn what's *really* going on in town.

Oh sure, you may have to read between the lines, but these little snippets from the police dispatcher and sheriff's logs are the haikus of Main Street, U.S.A. In major metropolitan areas, of course, the police and news media don't care about neighborhood squabbles and crimes so petty they barely rise to the level of "nuisance." Imagine how police in South L.A., for example, might react to this call that came into the Chadron, Nebraska, police dispatcher:

> RP [reporting party] from the 900 block of Morehead Street reported that someone had taken three garden gnomes from her location sometime during the night. She described them as plastic with chubby cheeks and red hats.

In a big city, not even all the *homicides* are considered newsworthy. But in a small town, no complaint is too small to be dutifully logged by a police dispatcher and then relayed—often word for word—by the local editor to his faithful readers. Week after week, the police blotter offers a brief glimpse behind the curtains of the community, showing the worst, and sometimes even the best, of its residents.

"Papers have always been in the business of dishing dirt," says Al Cross, director of the Institute for Rural Journalism and Community Issues (IRJCI) at the University of Kentucky. The police blotter, he says, allows the small-town paper to dish the dirt in the safe, dispassionate language of law enforcement, coupled with the unique conversational quality of the caller. It is a potent combination.

From Boonville, California:

4:54 p.m.—A Boonville resident said his neighbor was dangerously nuts.

6:34 p.m.—The Boonville resident said that his dangerously nuts neighbor was now yelling at him and throwing rocks at his house.

From Espanola, New Mexico:

11:17 a.m.—A caller said a man was either choking or hugging a woman parked at Valley National Bank. She said she wasn't sure what she saw but it seemed rough if it was a hug.

6:45 a.m.—A private drive 1625 caller said he just wanted to let someone know that the TV and everyone are spreading the wrong word. Officers were advised.

From Dutch Harbor, Alaska:

March 25—Ambulance request. EMS volunteers provided medical care to an intoxicated, belligerent man experiencing various body aches as a result of being struck by 2000 pounds of frozen fish product 24 hours earlier.

From Concrete, Washington:

September 21—A Hamilton caller reported waking up at night and finding an unidentified man sleeping on his couch in the living room. Caller said when the man woke up, he confronted him and the man walked out of the house. Visiting man smelled of intoxicants. Deputy asked homeowner why he waited until the next day to report this; man said he didn't think too much about it until now.

September 18—A Lyman caller reported that she suspected her 12-year-old son had stolen $80 from her purse. Caller said she confronted her son, who admitted taking the money and buying a Sony Play Station. Caller wanted advice on her options for how to deal with the boy.

From Chadron, Nebraska:

3:07 p.m.—RP stated his ex-neighbor drove by and flipped him off in the 200 block of North Mears.

6:52 p.m.—RP advised her neighbors in the 300 block of Pinecrest Drive were "wrecking my state of mind."

The editor of the *Chadron Record*, George Ledbetter, says his paper's "Police Beat" column rivals the obituaries in popularity and that he puts out "The Best of the Police Beat" in the last edition of the year. Police blotters often catch the attention of the outside world as well, mostly for their humorous insights into small-town life. David Letterman and Jay Leno make such items regular features on their talk shows, and several Internet sites are devoted to culling "the "best" blotter items from all over the country, where you can find items like these:

An Edgewood man reported recently that his wife had gone missing some 18 months ago.

Employees of Eckerd's reported about 12:25 a.m. Tuesday that two men came into the store, loaded birthday bags with "have a nice day" yellow faces on them with 52 tubes of vaginal anti-fungal cream, and left without paying. The cream was valued at $894.98.

I first heard about the *Chadron Record*'s "Police Beat" when *New York Times* reporter Dan Barry featured it in his column "This Land." "Over all," he wrote, "what emerges is a kind of weekly prose poem to the human condition, where annoyance about barking dogs is validated, where nighttime fears born of isolation are reflected, where concern about others is memorialized."

Chadron Record editor Ledbetter says neighbors in this small prairie town of 5,600 residents do look out for one another, although their concern is sometimes served up with a dollop of judgment.

RP stated that there is a 9-year-old boy out mowing the yard and feels that is endangering the child in doing so when the mother is perfectly capable of doing it herself.

RP advised her neighbor has two Chihuahuas and he's outside putting in an electrical fence. RP stated it looks like he's putting it underground but still that's going to be too much for those little dogs.

Ledbetter says the *Chadron Record* purposely leaves out names and specific addresses. "We don't feel the purpose of the 'Police Beat' is to identify individuals," he tells me, but even so, people can often figure out who is involved. And that can have serious blowback, despite the paper's efforts to protect the privacy of the callers. One woman who had called police to report possible child abuse next door was identified in the paper as "RP calling from the 200 block of Lake." "She called us, very upset," Ledbetter says, "to explain that there were only two houses on that block."

Child abuse and domestic violence are the darker side of the police blotters in small-town weeklies. And once in a while, a crime is big enough to rise up from the anonymity of the blotter to the spotlight of the front page. Ledbetter says a member of the school board was recently arrested for domestic assault while intoxicated, and was jailed. "He's got a bad drinking problem," says Ledbetter, "and we wrote about it, and some people were upset. But he's not just anybody, he's an official who is making decisions about how to spend taxpayer dollars."

But for the most part, he says, the blotter reveals the everyday realities of a community where police take the time to respond to all sorts of seemingly trivial calls. "One older lady," Ledbetter notes, "calls them almost every day and wants police to help her when her blood pressure goes up. And they roll out every time. Basically, she's just lonely." He says the paper stopped printing all her calls, but they did include one in the year's "best" list:

RP in the 400 block of Chapin advised that the batteries in her blood pressure machine are not working and is requesting an officer come over and change them for her.

A large percentage of the calls, says Ledbetter, have to do with animals, a category that includes two basic types of stories: animals in trouble and animals causing trouble.

RP requested assistance in the 300 block of West 10th in getting his overweight dog up the basement stairs.

RP on the 900 block of Parry Drive advised a squirrel has climbed down her chimney and is now in the fireplace looking at her through the glass door, chirping at her.

Animals, in fact, turn up with regularity in police blotters across the country. In Maine, the calls may involve reports of "moose in the road." In Alaska, critter crime is as varied as the wildlife. Consider this blotter item from Dutch Harbor, a port in the town of Unalaska (and home base for the TV show *Deadliest Catch*):

> Three juvenile boys phoned police and reported they had taken refuge inside a piece of playground equipment because they were in fear of imminent attack by a bald eagle. The suspect eagle hissed and puffed his chest feathers at the responding officer before flying from the area.

Sgt. Jennifer Shockley of the Unalaska Police Force wrote this particular item. Her weekly police report is carried in two weeklies: the *Unalaska Advertiser* and the *Dutch Harbor Fisherman*. Thanks to their Web sites, Shockley now enjoys a following around the world. The *Los Angeles Times* no doubt added to her base of fans (which now includes this one) after featuring her police reports in a front-page story. Shockley's writing style, often heavy with alliteration, is half the fun.

> A herd of hostile horses harassed a cyclist as he was riding his bike near Morris Cove. The complainant positively identified the suspect equine. The responding officer informed the cyclist that the stallions might be gelded soon, with resultant decreased testosterone levels and concomitant displays of aggressive behavior.

There is plenty of aggressive behavior from the human animals as well, something that might seem obvious in a port where thousands of fisherman from all over the world converge for shore leave. And the police activity report even includes calls from out of town. Far out of town.

A woman in California called and asked an officer to tell her husband's Unalaska mistress not to phone their house anymore.

But we digress. We're on the subject of critter crime, and no paper milks it more than the *Bisbee Observer* in Arizona. Each week, on the top of the front page, the editor includes a tease—"Inside: Police Beat"—followed by an alarming phrase about animals out of control. "Cat attacks children and dogs!" reads one. Turning to the "Police Beat" column inside, readers might be disappointed to learn that the "tease" is pretty much the whole story.

A woman in the 900 block of Headstart Way reported a cat attacking her children and dogs.

We never do learn what the cat's problem is, exactly, but there are dozens of other animal problems to divert the reader, from aggressive cows on the road to poisonous snakes in the bedroom. Outsiders might be a bit confused by repeated entries referring to the roundup of UDAS (as in, "a vehicle that stopped at Bisbee Beverage on Highway 92 was found to contain nine UDAS"). UDA stands for "undocumented alien," and this town on the Mexican border sees so many of them that the paper does not have room in the police blotter to spell out every arrest. Instead, it may print a summary, such as, "This week, Bisbee police located 106 UDAS and turned them over to Border Patrol agents."

That may sound callous, especially since immigrant rights groups consider the use of the word *alien* a dehumanizing slur. But such references can serve as a window into the local culture. In Bisbee, the debate over illegal immigration is not abstract. It is in their backyards, literally. Locals know better, for example, than to leave clothes on the line to dry overnight; they will be gone in the morning.

In Chadron, Nebraska, the in-your-backyard issue is the problem of poverty and alcoholism at the Pine Ridge Indian Reservation, which lies less than thirty miles away. The *Chadron Record*'s "Police Beat" reflects these social issues—and also the regional racism. "We print the calls as they come into the dispatcher," says editor George Ledbetter. "We don't rewrite them to make them politically correct. One caller reported to say there was 'a drunk Indian passed out in his yard and asked an officer to remove him so caller could continue mowing his lawn, without being forced to mow around the Indian.' There is plenty of racism here," he admits, "but our duty is to hold a mirror up to the community so it can change for the better."

And the sad truth for many rural towns is that alcohol and drug abuse are rampant, provoking a good portion of those calls to the police. In the words of Kevin Bersett, news editor for the *Rio Grande Sun*, "We seem to have a lot of people who do ridiculous things at all times of the day and night. Every week there's something. I feel bad for laughing at it, but it is funny."

The *Rio Grande Sun*, a weekly in the Espanola Valley in northern New Mexico, is a family-owned paper that has won many awards for its investigative reporting into local political corruption. "I like being someplace," says Bersett, "where the newspaper still matters." He notes that publisher Robert Trapp, who started the paper in the 1950s, "believes there should be a huge separation between the advertising side and the journalism side. You'll never get in trouble here," says Bersett, "for pushing too hard, pushing for records." The paper has often taken that battle to the courtroom, successfully suing the Los Alamos National Laboratory and the city of Espanola, among others, to force them to publish records they had attempted to hide from the public. One recent investigation by the *Sun* revealed that officials in the school district had been selling its cars at a private auction, providing low prices to friends and family.

With a staff of six reporters, the paper manages to cover a wide range of stories, and it has seen its circulation grow from a few hundred in the 1950s to more than 11,000 today. But for all the award-winning investigative work, it is the *Sun*'s police blotter that draws the most attention. People from all over the world log onto the paper's Web site to read about the latest shenanigans in Rio Arriba County.

> 7:42 a.m.—A Jackrabbit Trail caller said his cousin's girlfriend was breaking a car window. Police determined everyone on the scene was drunk, and that the cousin's girlfriend was breaking the windows to her own car, which is not illegal.

> 12:40 p.m.—A caller said someone swerving all over the road near Romero's Fruit Stand was eating tamales while driving. Deputies couldn't find her.

"It's amazing to me," says Bersett, "what some people are doing on a workday. They're hammered at noon." Or, in the case cited above, by eight o'clock in the morning. One man was arrested so often for public drunkenness, remembers Bersett, "that the police referred to him as 'the town's foremost drunk.'" The round-the-clock alcohol and drug abuse is a reflection, he says, of the high unemployment. "We're out in the middle of nowhere. People don't have jobs and they just sit around all day." Couple that, he says, with the fact that there are only two officers on duty from midnight to six o'clock in the morning in Rio Arriba County—an area the size of about 5,800 square miles—and only six officers during daylight hours, and "people know that they usually won't get into trouble because the response time is so long. There's just kind of a lawlessness out here," he adds, "which is good for the newspaper business but also depressing. The police think we are making fun of people, but these people are making fun of themselves with their behavior. We don't embellish."

9:28 pm—An intoxicated Chimayo man, wearing pajama pants with devils on them and a brown jacket, walked outside his house, put an 8-inch buck knife to his throat and threatened to kill himself, his wife told police. The man had apparently dropped the knife while trying to climb into the crawl space between his roof and ceiling by the time police arrived.

Suicide attempts, even bungled ones, are obviously emergency calls. But, says Bersett, "it's amazing to see how many resources are wasted on nonemergency calls." He points out that all the dispatch entries they print originated as 911 calls.

3:51 p.m.—A San Pedro teenager ran away from home because she didn't want to wash the dishes, her parents said.

5:03 p.m.—A woman said she arrived home to find her bedroom door kicked down but hardly anything missing. She told police all her videos were in a trash can and only a beer from the refrigerator was taken.

Bersett falls into that group of editors who believe in removing the names of those who call or those who are arrested. One reason for doing so, they say, is that some of the charges are later dismissed, and the paper does not have the resources to follow each small case through its conclusion. Another reason:

people might stop reporting crimes in their neighborhoods if they thought they would be identified as the "snitch" that called it in.

But a number of newspaper editors believe they should consistently report the names of those arrested. Benjy Hamm is the editorial director at Landmark Community Newspapers, a chain of fifty-six papers around the country, most of them weeklies. While he says he will not dictate the policies of these papers because his company protects local autonomy, he personally believes in giving names. "When I was an editor," he recalls, "I had people call and ask me if I could leave their names out of the blotters. And I said I would hope I would lose my job if I did that. We don't pick who shows up in the police blotter. Just because you're my friend doesn't mean I will ignore the law. It doesn't supersede my obligation to the readers."

IRJCI director Al Cross says that while naming names is the rule, many papers have changed their policies because of special circumstances. He cites the example of the *Anderson News* of Lawrenceburg, Kentucky, which used to run front-page mug shots of those arrested for driving under the influence. A new editor wanted to change the policy, but first he solicited feedback from the police and public. The police told him the photos had no deterrent effect on DUI arrests, so he decided to quit publishing the mug shots. Then a woman called to ask that her name not be printed in connection with her DUI arrest: she had simply been woozy after taking some prescribed medication, she claimed. This might seem like splitting hairs, or intoxicants, but the editor decided that such gray areas could lead to trouble. Now the paper prints only the names of people who are convicted.

Laurie Ezzell Brown, editor of the *Canadian Record* in the Texas Panhandle, believes in consistency. She always gives names.

But she also takes the time to follow up with the court logs, and she reports if charges are dismissed or sentences imposed. "Consistency equals credibility," she says. "Without that, you have nothing."

"Not all editors can follow the arrests all the way through the process," says Tonda Rush. She is the legal counsel and public policy director for the National Newspaper Association, which represents thousands of weeklies. "You've got to keep a running list of names and charges, and that's hard." And what if the police pass on incorrect information to the paper? "Not all states have the same laws protecting papers if the police are wrong," says Rush. The trend now, she adds, is away from naming names in the police blotter.

But there is another trend that worries her more. The press used to enjoy access to police arrest information under the principle of the public's "right to know," she explains. Now the police, backed by some court rulings, are withholding certain information unless there is a public "*need* to know." Big difference. Who defines that "need"? Two developments have encouraged the shift in practice, she says. First, the medical privacy protections in the federal Health Insurance Portability and Accountability Act (HIPAA) prevent reporters from calling up the ambulance EMTs or the hospital after an assault or accident and acquiring the names of the victims. The only place you can find that information, some of the time at least, is in the police dispatch log. "Back in the days when I was in a newsroom," remembers Rush, "these were handwritten or typewritten logs you could check. Now that everything is electronic, you need to get access to their computer records. And if they aren't in a mood to cooperate, that cuts off the public's information."

This change especially angers Kevin Bersett, at the *Rio Grande*

Sun. "The whole blotter thing has been a huge public records fight for us. We used to go to the Espanola Police Department and look at their printouts. Then they went to a computer, and they don't print that out." He is not really upset about being denied access to medical calls; he understands the HIPAA restrictions on privacy. But the police tried to restrict his access to the 911 center where the computer resides, and "we had to fight them over that because if we can't see the 911 calls, then we have to take the word of the police department. You're letting the police dictate what the public knows."

And what information might the police omit? "We want to know their response times," continues Bersett. "Without access to that log, we can't tell if police and fire respond quickly enough." He points to the example of a recent traffic accident in which a number of people were killed. "Looking back at the logs we saw that someone had called earlier that day to report a drunk driver at the wheel of this same car. The police never rolled on that call."

This sort of editorial oversight of the local police is fairly unusual, simply because many weeklies run on shoestring budgets and have only one editor and perhaps one or two reporters on staff. When editors Doug and Linda Funk bought the *Dove Creek Press* in Colorado, for example, they decided to carry on the police blotter policy of the previous editor, an approach they call "Just This Once." It started when this previous editor, who had always printed the names for arrests and tickets reported by the sheriff, got a tearful phone call from a Norwood woman. She begged the editor not to print her name for a speeding ticket she had received late one night driving from Dove Creek to Norwood. It seems she was worried that her husband would figure out she was seeing her old boyfriend (which she was) in

Dove Creek. "Well," answered the editor, "just this once." And so, for a time, if someone called with a good reason, the Funks didn't print the name. Just that once. These days, the Funks leave the names out of the blotter entirely, in the interest of fairness.

The *Press*, in addition to covering the tiny town of Dove Creek, also reports on the high mesa farm community of Egnar. The first settlers there wanted to call the town "Range," but the name was already taken, so they had to be content with spelling it backwards. At any rate, some years ago Egnar provided the *Dove Creek Press* with one of its more interesting "Sheriff's Roundup" items. A local rancher had lost control of his emu herd, and the sheriff's dispatcher was fielding reports from terrified and confused locals who had spotted strange creatures loping through their pastures at fairly high speeds. For those who know of emus only as crossword puzzle answers, and I was certainly one of those, these cousins of the ostrich are, in fact, powerful birds, despite their inability to fly. They can grow to be 6 feet 6 inches tall, can run up to speeds of 35 miles per hour, and are often cranky when cornered. Police have been known to resort to tasers to take them down. (Believe it or not, you can watch emu captures on YouTube.) Emus also look like something from the Jurassic Age (they have been linked to dinosaurs, in fact), so it's not hard to imagine the impression they left on unsuspecting locals who caught a glimpse of them streaking by in the night. A single emu footprint left behind in the pasture would be enough to get some rumors going, especially for those who had no inkling that a local rancher was raising the birds for their meat, oil, and leather.

The Great Emu Escape was chronicled in the sheriff's blotter in bits and pieces for three weeks running, until all the local specimens of the genus *Dromaius* were finally captured. This incident occurred some time ago, and so far no other animal antics have really compared in the Dove Creek area. These two entries from December 10, 2009, are fairly typical:

> A local resident called to report a dog possibly in distress. The officer who responded concluded that the dog did not want to be caught by the owner.

> A horse in the county wandered over to the neighbor's property and started causing problems with the resident horses. The trouble causer was sent home to a secure barn.

Perhaps the best police blotter items are the ones that, emu-like, leave something (or almost everything) to the imagination. From the *Chadron Record*:

> 10:29 a.m. RP advised someone was sneaking around the neighborhood with a cape and a hood.

> 1:29 a.m. RP advised that someone had rung the doorbell in the 500 block of Chadron Avenue and left a "round" something on the front step with "a light on it."

> 11:55 p.m. RP advised that around 9 p.m. tonight a male subject came into the 400 block of West Third dressed in black and was wearing a Halloween mask. RP stated he came in and looked at everyone, then left. RP stated she just wanted to report that.

From the *Anderson Valley Advertiser*:

> 10:45 a.m. A thin woman estimated to be 40–50 years old in a dark shirt, light blue Levis and "a pair of worn sandals" was sobbing so despairingly, so inconsolably, in front of the Anderson Valley Market that passersby were seen dabbing

handkerchiefs at their eyes, too. Who the woman was or what had happened to her is not known.

The blotter style, whether Episodic Emu or Hilarious Haiku, is best in its unvarnished form. Every now and then, a newspaper tries to put its own witty spin on this feature, to mixed results. The *Telluride Daily Planet* used to do this in its weekly "Cop Shop" column. A reporter would take the official dispatches and put his own spin on them, usually adding a mini-headline for each.

HIGHER EDUCATION: They teach a lot of things at Yale: readin', writin', 'rithmetic, ruling the world through an old-boy network of cronyism and inherited wealth. But one thing they can't teach is how to hike through Bear Creek. These Yalies hiked up Bear Creek into a snow field and—surprise!—got wet and cold. Dressed in shorts and t-shirts! Search and rescue members and a helicopter found the co-eds. One look at the cold, wet Ivy-Leaguers suggested that they would not have survived the night. Why they couldn't just reverse course and follow their tracks home is an eternal mystery even the brainiacs at Yale can't solve.

Police blotter purists would cringe. The whole joy of reading these fragments of truth is to dive between the lines and swim in the deep end of imagination. And we like to provide our own commentary. I would bet that the story about kids from Yale getting lost in the woods would have been much funnier told in the dispassionate language of the police dispatcher, not the snarky parlance of reverse snobbery. "Simple" beats "sarcastic" every time.

George Ledbetter of the *Chadron Record* believes that "every story you write, no matter how insignificant, is important to someone. Don't be condescending," he says, "because these are people just like you, with the same hopes and aspirations." In what might be called his golden rule of local journalism, Ledbetter believes in "writing about others as you would want to be written about yourself."

The good thing about police blotters, of course, is that no real writing is required. The entries speak for themselves. All the paper has to do is apply a bit of selective editing. In fact, the "golden rule" of police blotters might best be defined as "do unto others as they do unto themselves." Nothing illustrates this better than an entry from the "15 Funniest Police Blotters" at www.oddee.com:

1:14 a.m. Caller reports hitting an intruder in the head with an axe. Notes that intruder was "in the mirror."

CHAPTER SEVEN

Never Speak Ill of the Dead

Obituaries, along with the police blotter and high school sports, make up the holy trinity of local news. But if you are looking for the unvarnished truth about the life of someone who has just passed away, warts and all, stick to the *New York Times*. Not only do small-town newspapers sometimes leave out the warts, they occasionally perform cosmetic surgery on the deceased's entire life. No one sees much harm in this practice because almost everyone in town knows the true story, anyway, and would consider it bad manners to report unsavory facts while the family is grieving. Euphemisms thrive in the small-town obituary. If papa was a gambling man, for example, he might be remembered the way the *Concrete Herald* (Concrete, Washington) eulogized Mylard "Mike" Morley: "He loved his horses, playing the slot machines, and corresponding with Publishers Clearing House."

The families themselves write many of these obits. And some papers, primarily those owned by chains, are starting to charge families for the privilege. "I think that's an unfortunate development," says the University of Kentucky's Al Cross. "Obituaries taken as a whole tell the story of a place. These people led interesting lives. One hallmark of a weekly newspaper is that you get these full-length obits and learn their connections in the community. Not all families can afford to pay."

Whether they charge for the privilege or not, the local papers usually provide guidelines to the family on what should be included. The *West Valley View* in Buckeye, Arizona, which does not charge, even provides guidelines on what *not* to include:

Examples of phrasing we omit:
  —Gone to be with the Lord
  —Loved to golf
  —Survivors beyond immediate family (no nieces, uncles, friends, pets)
  —Survivors' spouses (no sisters-in-law, sons-in-law)

Usually, however, the guidelines are fairly loose (and suggest no editorial aversion, say, to God or golfing), which means that readers are treated to the sort of telling personal details that would be left out of a more straightforward obituary. Jason Miller, the editor of the *Concrete Herald* in Concrete, Washington, thinks those personal flourishes are part of the charm. The *Herald*'s obituaries are always written by the families, so there is a lot of "he went to be with the Lord" and "she was taken home to be with her heavenly Father." One of Miller's favorites came from the obituary of a local park ranger: "he left this earth to hike the hills of heaven."

But references to the afterlife are not nearly as important as the details of what the Funks of Dove Creek call "the dash"—the life lived between the dates of birth and death. Take this line from the obituary of Sally Frances Hazen, seventy-six, in the *Dove Creek Press*: "She enjoyed crochet, embroidery, and visiting with anyone that would sit a spell." Or another entry from same paper, on the death of eighty-seven-year-old physician Edward G. Merritt:

> His patients always came first. He had office hours seven days a week, and when he started, office calls were $2 a visit. Making house calls was routine for Dr. Merritt, 24 hours a day. "If they can't come to me, I'll go to them," he was heard saying. Once a week he drove the windy, dirt road to Rico to take care of the miners and their families. Dr. Merritt was never seen without his black medical bag, whether it be taking care of friends, strangers broken down by the side of the road, or at rodeos helping cowboys.

And this, from the *Freeman (SD) Courier*, on the death of ninety-five-year-old Sarah Glanzer: "Her kitchen, filled with aromas of fresh bread, noodle soup, duck and pickled watermelon, was a place one always felt welcome and the hospitality was great. Grandchildren loved to play softball, dominoes, and Rook with grandma. Conversations with her children and grandchildren always included the question, 'Is everyone OK?'"

This is just one paragraph in a lengthy obituary that was most certainly written by a loving family member with an eye, and nose, for the kind of detail that draws in the reader, creating an almost universal longing for the platonic ideal of "grandma." I am sure Sarah Glanzer had a few character flaws, as we all do, but her final tribute is a paean to perfection.

But not everyone is a fan of the form. "American obituaries," writes curmudgeonly editor Bruce Anderson of the *Anderson Valley Advertiser*, "are in their unintended way insults in their simplifications, their rosy makeovers of the lives of the departed, their embalmer's prose leaving unmentioned the complications, the heartache, everything that comes from life's full monte."

Anderson wrote that paragraph as part of a front-page obituary he authored on the death of his brother, Ken. It is beautifully written, with detailed anecdotes about his brother's athletic prowess and winning disposition. But since it is a three-dimensional portrait, it is also brutally honest.

> Ken had secret lives, and don't we all? Our family will not appreciate my saying he was lucky in love, serially lucky, and never happier than his last twenty years in Ukiah with the former Diane Zucker. In the middle 1970s Ken got into gambling, real gambling. . . . He became one of the millions of Americans feeding organized crime. I walked into his house in Ukiah one day as he placed $8,000 on NFL football games. "I hope you know what you're doing," I said, knowing full well that a teacher putting $8,000 down on information gleaned from the sports page was a teacher about to lose his house. Which is what happened. Ken was lucky to emerge with his kneecaps because he couldn't pay what he owed these people, and they were people who had to be paid. But everybody liked Ken. Even the mafia, lucky for him.

Bruce Anderson finds it impossible to whitewash an obituary, even that of his own beloved brother, because he is an uncompromising truth-teller. But precisely *because* he tells the truth, the reader can easily empathize—with loving someone who was both fabulous and flawed, and with the agony of watching him die. In Ken Anderson's case, we learn from the obituary, the cause was myelofibrosis, a condition in which the body stops producing blood cells. Anderson includes the details not only of Ken's living, but of his dying.

> Last Wednesday when I got to the hospital, Ken had been moved to "Palliative Care" on the 14th floor. I marveled at this

grisly lingual evasion of the true purpose of the venue, which was death, a last luxurious look out the big view windows at the most beautiful city in the world [San Francisco]. There were couches and big chairs and even a sports bar–sized television set, all the decadent amenities of a luxury box at PacBell. [Ken was a Giants fan.]

But Ken was gone, he was way past view windows and ball games on big screen television sets. He was breathing but he was gone, unconscious, his chest heaving the way it does just before the death rattle and the heart stops. I hoped to hell they'd loaded him up on the morphine, I hoped he went out not regretting anything, I hoped he went out as happy as he lived, confident that his children were well and safe, that Zito would turn it around and Ishikawa would be good at first base.

It is unusual to find the details of death, not to mention the less savory character traits of the departed, in small-town obituaries. When, for example, Dr. James Redd committed suicide in Blanding, Utah, following his arrest on charges of stealing Indian artifacts (see chapter 4), the family wrote the obituary and never mentioned the cause of death. But then, they didn't need to. Everyone in town knew the cause, and it had been a front-page story in the same issue. For families, it is important for the obituary to stand alone; it gets clipped for family scrapbooks and goes down in the archives as the official remembrance of the man's life.

Shannon Smithey, a political scientist at Westminster College, has done extensive research on the cultural insights provided by obituaries. "Obits," she says, "are about identity preservation. We have a strong norm of not speaking ill of the dead." In a case like James Redd, of course, that cultural taboo worked in his favor. "But that norm," adds Smithey, "also underlines that you are not in control of your story after you're dead." Although including the "cause of death" is de rigueur at the major metropolitan papers, she says, the local obituary may omit that detail. So she looks for clues in the "suggested donations" at the end. Phrases like "donations can be made to the Cancer Society" or—more telling—"donations can be made to Mothers Against Drunk Driving" can provide some insight into the reasons for the person's demise. Smithey remembers one obituary, picked up by Salon.com, in which a surviving husband suggested not a donation but an action. "His wife had really hoped she would live to vote in the 2004 election," says Smithey, "but since she didn't, he asked people to go out and vote against George Bush on her behalf."

Obituaries from small-town papers have almost as big a fan base as the police blotters. Columnist Caitlin Kelly, a former reporter for Toronto's *Globe and Mail* who blogs for trueslant. com, describes her addiction this way: "I read obits because so many strangers fascinate me. I read obits because I want to hear what others say about them and how they are remembered by those who knew and loved them best, not just those wealthy, powerful or famous enough to have a reporter call up and formally interview their colleagues or family. So often, I read an obit of a non-famous, non-wealthy person I've never heard of and think: 'Wish I'd met you. What a cool life. How loved you were!'"

It is easy to have that reaction when perusing obits from all over. The death of ninety-year-old native Alaskan Tom Nurauq Kasayulie, for example, prompted this memorial by his family in the *Tundra Drums*, a tribal newspaper printed in Anchorage, Alaska:

During the influenza epidemic when he was a boy, Kasa-yulie moved to the mountains where he became a reindeer herder and trapper along with people then called Laplanders. Kasayulie enjoyed the subsistence way of life—gathering, hunting, fishing and trapping. He taught the skills to his children and grandchildren. At 87, Kasayulie went on his last trip with family on the Kiseralik River. He disappeared during the trip. Son Joel feared he fell somewhere. Then Joel heard a faint voice in the distance and spotted him halfway up the mountain. Kasayulie wanted to continue to the summit, [saying] 'I feel young again and I don't feel old.' Kasayulie continued and said that his best medicine he ever had was climbing up that mountain.

Native American obituaries are much longer than most, in part because they generally name every single living relative as survivors of the deceased. A typical example, from the *Big Horn County News* in Hardin, Montana, is the obituary for Sheldon Dean Pickett (Crow name Bainniiitcschesh, or "Talks Good to Others"), forty-three, who died of injuries sustained in a fall. We learn that he was "a member of the Crow Community Baptist Church, Greasy Mouth Clan and was a Bad War Deeds child." He enjoyed participating in Sun Dances, peyote meetings, and sweat lodge ceremonies and "was an expert tepee builder." A long list of survivors follows, including members of the Pretty Paint, Plain Feather, Lion Shows, High Hawk, Long Ears, Woodtick, and Chief Goes Out families.

Another obituary in that same issue has a list of survivors so long that it takes up two pages. At the end, the family wrote, "Our family is very large; if we have missed you, please accept our apology."

Not all weeklies hand off the obituary writing to the family. The *Chilkat Valley News*, a weekly in Haines, Alaska, for example, had the good sense to give that job to reporter Heather Lende, who has lived in this small town all her adult life. In her book *If You Lived Here, I'd Know Your Name: News from Small Town Alaska*, Lende chronicles the lives and deaths in this small village at the northern tip of the Inside Passage.

"Death is a big part of life in Haines," she writes. "This is a dangerous place. One man died falling off a cliff while goat hunting. Another was lost diving for sea cucumbers. Skiffs capsize in icy water, planes disappear in the mountains. Sometimes people vanish without a trace."

Dealing with death is necessarily swift, at least in the practical sense. "Most people can't afford to pay to have the body flown out of a town to a place where it can be cremated," Lende tells me. "And since there is no funeral parlor in Haines, and no embalming, burial has to take place within three days." But in a town where everyone knows the deceased, funerals are community affairs. The high school gym was packed for the funeral of a popular basketball coach, she says, and the pastor invited everyone to come up in front of the coffin "and sink a basket for Jesus."

"I love what I do," says Lende. "Being an obituary writer means I think a lot about loss, but more about love. . . . Writing about the dead helps me celebrate the living—my neighbors, friends, husband, and five children—and this place, which some would say is on the edge of nowhere, but for me is the center of everywhere."

Haines, Alaska, like any other small town, has its fair share of eccentric characters. One such figure was a one-legged gold miner named Josephine "Porcupine Jo" Jurgeleit, a talented storyteller, albeit a bit of a profane and irascible one. She got her nickname because she owned one of two active placer mines on Porcupine Creek. The Schnabel family owned the other.

"Jo threatened to settle most of her disputes with a rifle," writes Lende in her book, "and just about all of them were with John Schnabel over mining claims. For years, Jo kept up a running feud with the Schnabels. The bullets she fired whizzed past John's head on many otherwise still woodland evenings. When she failed to kill him, she took John to court. John says he never had much of a chance against 'a one-legged widow'—even if she was well known for her grit and independence."

But Lende did not include all those details when it came to writing Jurgeleit's obit some years later. Instead, she managed to paint a picture of her by quoting friends and relatives. Jo's sister Jane, for example, put it this way: "Many of Josephine's stories were risqué, and her language was colorful." Lende says using quotes is a useful technique for putting "something that some people might consider a criticism into an obituary that you want the family to still be able to clip and save. You get someone who loved the deceased to say it. Then it becomes a compliment."

Getting people who loved the deceased to provide details that go beyond the usual posthumous platitudes is not easy, but Lende's willingness to spend time with the families, plus the fact that she lives in the same small town and can feel real empathy for their loss, elicits three-dimensional portraits that make even an outsider wish they had known the person. Take this obituary for eighty-five-year-old Robert "Bob" Stickler in the January 7th, 2010, issue of the *Chilkat Valley News*:

> "He was humble, quiet, and a perfectionist," said son Dave Stickler, noting that his mother did most of the talking for the pair.

A father of eight, Stickler supported his family working on metal projects large and small, from fabricating pipelines for local fuel companies to repairing a utility trailer in his backyard shop. "For years he fixed everything in town. He was the guy we all went to," said Tim Maust.

Dave Stickler said no project was too small or large. "If you were on a broken down spaceship, he's one of the guys you'd want with you."

We also learn that Stickler served in the Army Air Corps during World War Two and had been instrumental in the Battle of Saipan, manufacturing manifolds so the trucks could be submersible. That is obviously noteworthy, but Lende tells me she would not have known about it if she had not pushed the family to say more than their initial statement of "He was a proud World War Two vet."

"You've got to get them to be specific," she says, and get them to tell detailed stories that move beyond bland generalities. "That should be true whether you're writing about Bob Stickler or Patrick Swayze," she continues, "but I am amazed at how many professional publications, like *People*, write obituaries that are so trite they all sound the same."

When Stickler's friends told her, for example, that he was generous with his talents, she pushed them for real stories to illustrate that point, such as this one: "Nishan Weerasinghe recalled volunteering to fix a snow machine trailer for a single mother, but the project was beyond his skills, so he took it to Stickler. "Bob worked on that thing for about eight hours, it was in bad shape, and when he got done he asked who it was for, and I told him, and he said, 'Tell her it's on the house.'"

The more difficult cases, says Lende, involve that "too close for comfort" factor which comes with writing about people you know well. When she learned that electrician Glenn Henrichs had died, she had no trouble finding people who could praise his skills in entertaining stories.

Fellow electrician Erwin Hertz worked with Henrichs on the remodel of the Chilkat Center, and said his expertise exceeded that of electrical engineers. Hertz said the company that manufactured the sound board system sent the engineer who designed it from Atlanta to help install it. "He was in the white suit and tie, very professional looking and all business."

But when they couldn't get the system to work, Hertz called Henrichs, who arrived looking like he had slept in his truck. "He looked horrible. His tennis shoes had holes in them, and he had no socks, and the fleece was all tore out of his jacket. That engineer looked at him like he had leprosy."

After spending all night reading sheets of electrical blueprints, Hertz said Henrichs asked them for a phone. He took it apart, removed a small piece and soldered it onto a part of the soundboard. It worked.

"After that, the engineer followed him around like a puppy dog," Hertz said.

If Lende had ended it there, with this amusing story about Henrichs's amazing talent as an electrician, she realized she would not be telling the whole truth. She knew the reason the man looked so disheveled and horrible, and not just on this occasion, was because of a terrible traffic accident that had changed his life, plunging him into depression. "I called his sister in Juneau to tell her that we wanted to include the information about the accident in the obituary and the sister was dead set against it. But my editor, Tom Morphet, insisted. He said if the sister wanted to control the obituary, she could pay a hundred dollar fee and write it herself." The sister declined that offer and Lende added this paragraph near the end of the obituary: "In 1983, Henrichs was the driver in a collision that seriously injured his stepdaughter and killed a friend of hers. Although Henrichs was found to not be at fault, the accident weighed heavily on him, friends said."

Lende's obituaries are honest but tempered by compassion. And she admits she would be guilty of the "dishonesty of omission" if her editor were not such a stickler for the truth in obituaries. One of her most difficult assignments was an obit she wrote for Arne Olsson, a former member of the Haines City Council and a tourism entrepreneur who had operated a beautiful old historic hotel, among other businesses. Most of the obituary consists of praise for his marketing skills and examples of Olsson's gregarious nature. Former tourism director Susan Bell praised Olsson for "marketing Haines, the region, and all of Alaska from his unique position of being a host, tour guide and a local. He called himself a roofer, because he covered everything—from driving the bus to greeting the guests."

Many paragraphs later, after relating that Olsson was a self-taught plumber, electrician, carpenter, cook, and locksmith, not to mention an instrument-rated pilot, Lende finally divulges what she had only hinted at in the first paragraph, which mentions that Olsson had died of liver failure at the age of fifty-five. He had struggled with alcohol addiction. "We all loved Arne, and there really wasn't anything he couldn't do when he put his mind to it, but time and again the disease that is alcoholism pulled him away, and in the end, it killed him," in spite of efforts to save him, lifelong friend Steve Schaffer said.

And then she added another quote, one clearly intended to

bring the reader back to the man's essence, so that his disease would not, in the end, define him. "Friend Tony Tengs said 'Arne had a soft side for all his forthrightness; he could speak his mind, [but] there was a real sweetness, a real gentleness about him.'"

In a small town, "pillars of the community" are defined by their actions, the daily kindnesses that affect their neighbors' lives. Arne Olsson and Bob Stickler certainly qualified, whatever their personal demons. And, according to Lende, so did Tom Ward, the first Euro-American to live his entire life in Haines. He had four children with his first wife and inherited about a dozen stepchildren and step-grandchildren from his second wife. "It seems," says Lende, "that he was related in one way or another to half the people in town." And almost all the people in town loved him, even though his "career" was cutting, splitting, and selling wood.

Lende had a difficult time getting Ward's friends to put their admiration into words. One longtime pal, Leo Smith, sat at Lende's kitchen table "with his cap in his hands, and started to tell me about his last moose hunt with Tom, but he stopped mid-sentence. Then Leo, this tough, gentle old logger, started to cry. I didn't know what to do. Leo stood up, wiping his wet face with a bare hand and said, 'Tom was a good friend, you can print that in your paper. He was a darn good friend.' And he walked out the door."

When Lende finally turned in her obituary for Tom Ward, it ran two pages long, and her editor roared, "Jesus, Heather! The guy was a woodcutter, not the governor."

Then he put it on the front page.

The front page of the weekly newspaper is the final resting place for the lives of "pillars of the community." Editor M. E. Sprengelmeyer of the *Guadalupe County Communicator* in New

Mexico says "obits are critical for us." In one recent issue, he notes, "we had *six* obits in our little paper"—quite a few if you consider the size of the town. "So we ran a full page of obits inside, plus the Sheehan story on page one. Above the fold."

The "Sheehan story" was the obituary for David Sheehan, "an East Coast native who became a pillar of the Santa Rosa community. The 75-year-old retired businessman and tireless community volunteer died on Monday, Jan. 4 [2010] at his home in Santa Rosa."

It's not easy earning "pillar" status in a small western town when you are from the East Coast. But we learn that Sheehan "had so immersed himself in the everyday affairs of Guadalupe County that it would be easy to forget that he was not an area native, and that he split his time between here and Virginia."

The obit lists Sheehan's major contributions: sitting on the hospital board, contributing to the renovation of a historic Catholic church. But it's the details, given in the words of local friends, that bring the man to life for someone who never knew him.

"'He was a good—a great man,' said close friend Cecilio Page. 'Look at all the help he gave Santa Rosa. He was the one pushing on the [St. Rose Church] project. He had just bought the lighting system. He planted all the trees around the church. It's going to be a great loss. I don't think words can describe the loss. He was good people.'"

"Good people" is a category higher than mere philanthropist. The sort of "status" information that might form the basis of obituary headlines at major papers gets less print space here, including the fact that Sheehan had worked at Mobil Oil for more than thirty years and reached the position of "General Manager of Corporate Aviation." He was also a large landowner and was planning to start a winery in his adopted home.

In other words, the way a person is remembered in a small town has very little to do with wealth or career achievements. Instead, it depends on the daily interactions that define a person's character. Sheehan and friends had been working on restoring the church bell tower, prompting his "close amigo Horacio Lopez" to say, "We're going to ring the church bell there for the first time in years." A simple detail, delivered in simple words by a loving friend, is much more powerful than an overwrought attempt at exaltation. Simple beats sentimental every time in obituaries, just as simple beats sarcastic in police blotters.

That is not to say that local obituaries are sugar-free. Far from it. One of the most sentimental obituary writers in the annals of small-town newspapering was Dan Hunter, who founded the *Dove Creek Press* in 1940. According to the book *Unforgettable Characters of Western Colorado* by Al Look, Hunter was known as the Sage of the Sagebrush and a wordslinger whose obituaries were quoted across the nation by national publications, including the *New Yorker*. "All he had for experience," wrote Look, "were words. And Dan Hunter knew a lot of words. In fact, he was perhaps the most prolific word-merchant of his generation. He could use more words to say nothing than any editor alive, and that is a considerable statement." Obituaries, in particular, were rife with flowery description. "He never used one word," wrote Look, "when ten would do," adding, "Hunter made it almost a pleasure to die." An example:

In life Anita scattered her blossoms far and wide as she went from place to place doing good. Now she rests where love and bliss immortal reign. She was never solitary when alone, for the flowers nodded gaily when she passed their way, wayside brooks slipped laughingly by as she trod their shores, birds sang lyrics as she counted their eggs. The winds were her companions as she roamed the hills, and the clouds, glorious sun and twinkling stars were symbols of her beauty and charm. We all shiver under the cold touch of death, but why grieve for her, for now she rests on a golden throne and forgets to weep.

And that is just the half of it. It goes on in this oleaginous style for several more coma-inducing paragraphs. Dan Hunter, in other words, was everything Bruce Anderson would detest. Not that Hunter wanted for literary critics in his own time. One editor, according to author Look, "called his obituaries 'profound nonsense.' Another said 'the gentleman is intoxicated with the exuberance of his own verbosity,' adding that he was 'good enough to be amusing and not bad enough to excite pity.'"

But Dan Hunter was not writing for the critics. He was writing for the ranchers and farmers and merchants who lived in and around Dove Creek. Look tells a story about the day "a grizzled old rancher walked in and plunked down cash for a subscription and said he wanted to take the paper because he liked to read 'them pieces you write about folks when they die.' Dan never did know if the man liked to see people die, or if he liked the decorated language in praise of the departed."

Actually, Hunter's motivation was equal parts poetic (I use the word loosely) and practical. Look says the editor had two reasons why he wrote such long obituaries: "One, he would have told you that when a person died he deserved to have some nice things said about him. Two, he set them to fill a hole he had in the page of type. And if he had a hole and no death, he would compose a piece about spring or some abstract subject."

Obviously, filling that hole week after week can become so routine that the art of obituary writing gets lost under deadline pressure (giving new meaning, really, to *deadline*). But when someone prominent in the community passes away, most editors still take the time to do justice to that person's life. A couple of my favorite examples come from my hometown newspaper, the *Norwood Post*.

One obituary is for eighty-five-year-old Dan Dillon, who died in a rollover accident on a mountain pass called Dallas Divide, a notoriously tricky spot that has claimed a number of lives over the years. Under the headline "A Full and Generous Heart," we learn that Dillon had touched almost everyone's lives during his seven decades in this small Colorado town. Some excerpts:

"We lost a ray of sunshine," says Norwood's Happy Belly Deli owner Julie Thorneycroft. "Every time he walked in that door, I just couldn't help but smile."

Jessica Hendricks, a Happy Belly Deli employee, has been in Norwood for just a few months, but "he made himself known. He'd sit in the corner and eat his ham sandwich, talk about life and give out hugs."

Sheila Henderson, one of Dan's neighbors, smiles as she says, "Even our animals loved him. They knew the sound of his car, his voice and came running. . . . He would climb right up and over the corral fence" to take care of the cows at their place.

"Dan has been in every play we've produced here," [local playwright] Kristina Stellhorn boasts. She gave him free reign to improvise his lines, because "he would always make up something funny."

We also learn from the *Norwood Post* obit that Dan played Santa Claus for the local kids every Christmas, was adopted by the preschool as their "official grandpa," and served as Scout Master for generations of Norwoodian Boy Scouts. He received the final honor of having his picture posted on the wall in the Happy Belly Deli above a sign reading, "We love you and will miss you, Dan."

This is the Norwood equivalent of a twenty-one-gun salute.

Another obituary in the *Norwood Post*, for the clerk of San Miguel County, confers the highest praise possible right up top, in the headline:

Doris Ruffe, as local as they come, dies at 76.

Doris Ruffe shuffled through the San Miguel County Clerk's office for the past 26 years, in pants cut just above the tops of her Keds, her face sometimes hinting she was up to something. Always. And now she's gone.

Ruffe is forever revered here; she is as local as they come, the best of what San Miguel County can produce. Her charm was her work ethic, her ability to do everything at once.

She had a sweet distrust in waves of technology; she preferred her molehills of papers to a hard drive.

And, while in her mid 70s, she took her own car door off, took that door apart and got her window to work right again.

She worked. Hard.

She never married and was quiet socially, preferring to keep to herself. "How can I say this? Doris never married. I always felt she was lonely," [former county clerk] Gay Cappis said. "She cared a lot about people. She seemed to always want to be doing something for somebody to fulfill her life. And she did. I just don't know how else to say it.

The obituary runs five columns wide. And in the middle, inside a box, one featured quote summarizes a life: "She cared a lot about people."

Imagine seeing *that* in the *New York Times*.

CHAPTER EIGHT

School Sports

Holy Hyperbole!

There is no such thing as understatement on the sports page of a small-town newspaper. Overstatement is the stuff of myth, and mythmaking is the job of the local sports writer. Oh, sure, one has to report scores, those annoying facts that get in the way of a good story, but they never stop a determined dream-weaver.

"One doesn't have to look outside our town to find greatness," begins a story about the middle school girls' volleyball team in the *Concrete Herald*, a weekly in Washington. It is an interesting claim, given that we learn later in the article that the team posted a 2-7 season. The same paper had a similarly optimistic spin on the girls' basketball team: "The Lady Lions finished January with a 4-12 record overall. The Lady Lions are a young group of ladies who show great intensity for 32 minutes."

But we're talking dreams here, and local sports is all about heroic tales of overcoming adversity, about a small town taking aim at the Goliath over in the next county. Every now and then, a local team actually produces a bona fide David to lead the charge. And when a star athlete meets a talented writer, the outcome can make for delightful reading. Reilly Capps, a reporter for the *Telluride Daily Planet*, described a high school basketball star in this way:

> Shocking fact: Michael Mathews could dunk in the eighth grade.
>
> Now, as a junior just a hair over 6 feet, he can dunk just about any way he wants: alley-oop, reverse, over a chair, in your face. All of which is fun to watch unless you're trying to defend him, in which case it's 31 Flavors of humiliation.
>
> Add to that his pinpoint shooting and quick hands, and the point guard has become the fifth leading scorer in Colorado, averaging 28 a game.
>
> Growing up in southern California, where basketball is practically a religion, Mathews developed into the best player Telluride has seen, possibly ever.
>
> In the past, the Miners basketball team had seen slightly more wins than the Kenyan national ski team.

Capps goes on to credit the coach as well as another rising star on the team: "Ian MacCracken, a kid so tall they ought to put in a fire escape, is usually the Miners' second-leading scorer. He spends so much time at the gym that he ought to pay rent there, and his rebounding—only Windex is more effective at cleaning glass."

I don't follow sports reporting all that carefully, but my guess is that this is fairly original stuff. Of course, when I'm searching for anything "original," I always turn back to Bruce Anderson, Mendocino County's resident curmudgeon. And even in the arena of sports, he does not disappoint. He is especially thrilled when a pair of streakers enlivens the high school's Homecoming festivities during the football game's halftime.

The boy was completely nude. And spectacularly acrobatic. He *cartwheeled* across the field as the girl, who wore the bottom half a swim suit, followed him in a kind of lateral jumping jack. Spectators overwhelmingly enjoyed the prank, especially when high school principal Jim Tomlin and Ag teacher Beth Swehla vainly attempted to chase the two down, not that either of the teen nudists seemed particularly intent upon eluding either identification or capture. A sideline crew of eight or ten more high schoolers had also planned to streak the event but contented themselves with cheering on their two champions. We hope rumors that the two pranksters might suffer periods of expulsion are untrue. The crowd enjoyed the heck out of it. Of course, nude dashes by the nubile across the high school fields of play would certainly draw large crowds if they were incorporated into high school events, but we're probably a few years away from official sanction. But go for it, kids, go for it while you're young and beautiful, go for it before you become like the rest of us, walking around like we'd been hit with baseball bats wondering what the hell happened. Resist! Always!

Anderson is a reality-based booster, but a booster nonetheless. In one article, he gently chides Boonville residents for the sparse attendance at high school basketball games.

Stopped in at the Boonville gym Monday night for a look at the Panther basketball teams as they took on visiting Fort Bragg, a much larger school. Coach Brian Wyant's Lady Panthers, I would say, seem to have grasped the basics of the game *in theory*, but will undoubtedly improve as the season continues. Our girls were no match for Fort Bragg, succumbing to the Coast ladies, 52–26. The male-type Panthers came roaring out and, with Justin Johnson banging in a couple of early three-pointers . . . darned if the Panthers didn't have Fort Bragg down much of the game, only failing at the end of the last quarter via some unwise fouls. . . . The visitors, by the way, brought more spectators than Boonville seemed able to muster. This year's teams hustle, they're competitive, mucho fun to watch, and certainly much more entertaining than anything you're likely to see on television in the same time slot.

The use of the word *lady*, by the way, is ubiquitous in the naming of girls' teams in small towns, perhaps a throwback to a time when girls' sports were, at best, an afterthought. And certainly the "ladies" moniker must get tiring when writing about a whole group of them in one article, as Scott Boyle had to do in the *San Juan Record*, the weekly in Monticello, Utah.

> Let's talk volleyball for a change, shall we? They say that losing is dreadful, losing to a Sevier school is severe, but losing to both Seviers, North and South, is dreadfully severe.
>
> The Lady Broncos found themselves in just such a predicament with losses to the Lady Rams and the Lady Wolves in the past 10 days.

By the time Boyle gets around to describing a team from yet another high school, his frustration is showing.

"McKenzie, a 6′1″ sophomore, is having a breakout year for the Lady Cavemen (or is it Cavewomen?)."

The real frustration for local sportswriters, of course, is not so much what's in a name, but what's on the scoreboard. When the home team is struggling, it leaves the reporter grasping to find something, anything, positive to say.

In Santa Rosa, New Mexico, the Lions football team was off

to a dismal start in the 2009 season. Even so, editor M. E. Sprengelmeyer managed to find the pony in the proverbial pile. His headline put the best possible spin on the local team's loss:

Lions Show Signs of Life in Loss #2

With two seconds left on the clock on Friday, the purple-decked crowd at Santa Rosa High School rose to its feet roaring, stomping, ringing cowbells and hoping.

The last play seemed meaningless. The Lions already trailed 35 to 19 to the Tularosa Wildcats, whose aerial assault was constant, consistent, and devastating.

But the crowd was hungry for something, anything, to get excited about after eight mostly lackluster quarters to open the 2009 season and Mario Trujillo's tenure as head coach.

They snapped the ball. They tried. The play fell short. And as the local fans went to the exits, Tularosa's road crew swarmed to the field to dance on the Lion's home turf.

The Lions are in a fight to keep their win-hungry fans interested. In the fourth quarter, when the Wildcats connected on a 61-yard pass for their final score, many Santa Rosa fans started heading to the exits with nearly 4 minutes still left on the clock.

"Hey, where are all you guys going?" one diehard fan yelled angrily. "Sit down and support your team."

As any journalist knows, the final quote can have a lasting impact. And while the reporter cannot come right out and scold the fans (unless, of course, that reporter is Bruce Anderson), he can certainly let the quote do it for him. Not to mention the choice of visuals. On the front page above the article headline is a photo of the fans—not the team—in action, cheering and ringing cowbells.

As luck would have it, the following week marked a dramatic turnaround for the Santa Rosa Lions. They defeated the Hot Springs Tigers 40–0, a complete rout. This time, the front page featured a photo of the players as well as a dramatic retelling of the game's highlights, right down to the last play.

> Trujillo, who was 0-2 to start his run as head coach, pulled his defense into a huddle with the clock stopped at 34 seconds, the ball on the 16 yard line.
>
> Whatever he said, the purple huddle broke with new intensity, and the coach calmly walked back to the sidelines.
>
> The teams squared off at the line of scrimmage. At the snap, the quarterback dropped back to pass, with big pressure from the Lions' line. The ball went in the air. The pass appeared to be tipped. It wobbled.
>
> The ball ended up in the arms of Lions' defender Dylan Bradley, big number 52, who took the surprise interception and went rumbling and stumbling down the sidelines, right in front of his ecstatic coaches and teammates, until he ran out of gas and was tackled just short of what would have been the most improbable score.
>
> The fans in the grandstands roared like Mighty Lions are supposed to roar. The cowbells clanked in jubilation. Senior starters led a purple mob around the unlikely hero of the shutout: the junior, Bradley.
>
> It was only one win, and against a team that's now winless at 0-3. But that could have been the Lions if they hadn't learned the lessons of the first two games of the season.

You do not have to be Dylan Bradley's parents to be hooked by this vivid replay, although you can bet they bought extra copies of the paper that week. I have never met Bradley or any of the other Lions, for that matter, but as a subscriber reading from afar, I found myself waiting for the next installment. And, like a fan of the television series *Friday Night Lights* (which I am), I was not disappointed.

District Champs: Lions Storm to State

The Santa Rosa Lions didn't just steamroll the Tucumcari Rattlers last Friday night. With a 53–7 victory that was a shutout until the very last tick on the clock, they seized the District 2AA Championship and silenced the naysayers who kept fretting over the season's slow start.

"When we started out at 0 and 2, nobody thought we could do it," star linebacker Chris Sanchez proclaimed as he stormed in and out of the post-game locker room still wearing a fierce game face. "We proved 'em wrong. We proved 'em wrong!"

Indeed they did. The Lions ended their dramatic comeback season 7-2, and champions in their division. All those names and all those photos, week after week, sold a lot of papers. And ads.

No one appreciates that formula better than Jason Turner, the sports reporter for the *Canadian Record*. "In Texas, and in Canadian," he says, "there are two seasons: football season and waiting-for-football season." He says the TV show *Friday Night Lights*, in which life in a small Texas town revolves completely around the high school football team, "is an understatement. They live and breathe it here."

When I visited Canadian, I could not help but notice how impressive the football stadium was for a town of this size. The team's division includes school districts with enrollments between 200 and 400 students. "There are only 196 kids in the high school," says Turner, "but they'll have 40 or 50 kids go out for the team. Kids aren't forced to play, they grow up *wanting* to play."

Which is why, he explains, voters did not hesitate to pass a bond issue to build an impressive field house. The field itself is covered in Astroturf and surrounded by enormous lights. He hastens to add, however, that "the voters also approved a bond issue to remodel the middle school auditorium and provide every kid with a laptop computer."

But it is football that binds the community together. "Friday night is everything," he says. "When we have out of town games, the whole town shuts down so people can go." And when the Wildcats play at home, there is an elaborate ritual for starting each game. First, the crowd observes a moment of silence and recites the Pledge of Allegiance. Then each school gets to sing its fight song, which also serves as the cue for the smoke machine to start up. Students carry out a giant inflatable head of a wildcat that emerges dramatically out of the smoke. Finally, the team kneels down in prayer. Then, and only then, can the game begin.

Only the Lady Wildcats basketball team gets anything close to that sort of attention, says Turner, because they are also a winning team. There are not enough boys in the school to field both a championship football and basketball team, so the girls get the glory. At the beginning of each game, the lights go off in the gym, and each girl is introduced under a spotlight as an announcer calls out their names and positions in a dramatic tone of voice.

Turner loves every detail.

"When I was younger," he recalls, "I thought I wanted to make a lot of money. But now, peace of mind and the sense of community is what count. And I have the best job in the world. They pay me to watch football!"

"They" is editor Laurie Ezzell Brown, who used her column "Field Notes" to express her gratitude to Turner for deciding to join her tiny staff. He moved to the Panhandle in 2006 to be with his girlfriend. As Laurie wrote,

When an Oklahoma City boy first caught the attention of our office manager's daughter, I did not realize that fate was intervening. When he moved to Canadian, though, and brought his lifetime love of sports and an uncanny ability to remember every score, every stat, and every jersey number of every player in nearly every sport known to man, I was smart enough to know I'd caught a break and had better not be foolish enough to let it go by. What neither Jason Turner nor I realized when I hired him as a part-time sportswriter was that Canadian High school's athletics program was about to write a few chapters of its own in the school's history books.

Part-time quickly morphed into full-time, though I wondered a time or two if it was crazy to add a full-time sportswriter to a payroll that was already stretched paper-thin.

Given the public's inherent hunger for sports, and for a team it can follow to the near ends of the earth, I took that gamble—a gamble that has paid off in increased reader interest and enthusiastic advertiser support. Seems the public does still read newspapers, if the newspaper offers them something worth reading.

And it certainly did not hurt that the football team had back-to-back state championships in their division in 2007 and 2008. The Wildcats also went to the finals in 2009 and lost, a setback that sent "people into a depression that lasted for weeks," says Turner.

It was especially painful, he adds, because the game was close and the Wildcats had a chance to win. "But the ref gave a touchdown to the other team after their player had clearly stepped out of bounds, then came back in to run for the touchdown. That call is all people talked about." The final score: 29–25.

"I had to be fair in my write-up," says Turner, "and say that the other team really did play better." But the pain of the loss was so acute that Laurie decided to complement Turner's objective reporting with an editorial comment.

> We would have wished it otherwise, certainly. But with Saturday's heartbreaking loss to Goldthwaite in the 1A State Championship game at Lubbock, we did learn something new about this Canadian Wildcat team: that they are as graceful and gracious in defeat as they have so often been in victory.
>
> The loss can't have been easy . . . not for the coaches or players, nor for the loyal fans. That it was a monumentally long drive back home to Canadian that night is certain.
>
> But the Wildcats' demeanor on the turf—from the opening kickoff to the final trophy presentation at midfield—was without blemish.
>
> Winning is relatively easy. Losing with such dignity after having played so well—now that's a championship season.

Being an objective sports reporter in such a charged atmosphere is sometimes a challenge, says Turner. "I get a lot of 'You never cover my son—he's an offensive lineman!' and 'Why don't you cover junior varsity more?'" And even though "the coach is a great guy and gives me complete access," he informs me, "I choose not to sit in on team meetings. I've got to keep that line clear: I'm not there as a fan."

Turner is so committed to that journalistic principle, in fact, that he never wears (and does not even own) Wildcat t-shirts or hats. He turns down invitations to go to the booster dinners. "I do have a Wildcat mug in my house that was given to me," he concedes, "but that's all I have."

Given his editor's reputation as a crusader committed to high ethical standards, I asked him if Laurie Ezzell Brown had instructed him to keep his distance from the team he covers. "Laurie didn't have to tell me," he says, "I just knew it was right. You don't become part of the story. I don't want to become friends with these kids. There is a mutual respect. I have a job to do. Do I root for them? Probably, on the inside."

Once, just once, his inner Wildcat broke loose. "Laurie did get a photo of me signaling a touchdown from the sidelines at the first championship game," he says. "Then she posted that photo in the office with a sticky note saying 'objective reporting at its best.'"

The Wildcats hand him plenty of material with which to work and keep the stories flowing, he says. The coach, Kyle Lynch, likes to pump up his team with a motivational speech that revolves around the slogan "212 degrees." He points out that while water is hot at 211 degrees, it produces steam at 212 degrees, enough to power a large locomotive. "If you guys can play at 212 degrees," he tells them, "things will heat up and you'll accomplish great things. You'll make history!"

And so the Canadian crowd chants "212! 212!" at every game, and the kids all sport "212 degree" stickers on their faces. Call it the equivalent of Dumbo's feather: all that matters is what they *think* matters. As one fan wrote in a letter to the editor, "This 212 attitude was important because the Wildcats were underdogs a lot. They were picked to finish third in their district and had never been to a State Championship game. They were often the least talented team on the field. A 212-degree effort allowed the Wildcats to overcome significant obstacles and accomplish the impossible."

The writer, a former resident now working for the Coca Cola Company in Plano, said he was so inspired by the "212" idea that he is using it to motivate his sales staff. "If a bunch of kids from the Texas Panhandle can accomplish the impossible through significant belief and effort, so can we!"

Given the almost reverential accolades garnered by the coach for this winning strategy, you can imagine how townspeople reacted when they heard that he might be leaving his coaching job. And Turner was among the first to get the tip.

"I'm sitting at a basketball game," he says, "and a school board member texted me to ask if I had seen the board's agenda. Seemed the school superintendent would be announcing his retirement. That meant that the assistant superintendent, who also happens to be the football coach, would be the likely successor. And that meant the team would soon need a new coach. I started telling people around me in the stands, and in a matter of seconds, it had spread through the gym."

"I call that the Hillbilly Twitter," he laughs. When it comes to any development affecting the football team, he tells me, all you need is word-of-mouth.

And all the *Canadian Record* needs to boost sales are those special editions touting the high school champs. Even when they are *not* champs, in fact, the Wildcats sell papers, something Laurie gratefully acknowledged in her column.

> I've gone all around the barn now just to say how much I appreciate both those loyal readers who circle the block every week waiting for us to fly the green flag upon arrival of each edition, and those faithful advertisers who've ponied up without complaint for every congratulatory and good luck page we've pitched their direction. In doing so, they have enabled us to

stay in business, to keep following and reporting the news of this community, and to pay our fine staffers a living—if not hog-high—wage.

We are grateful. I am grateful.

And so is Jason Turner, who never planned to be a sports reporter, much less make his home in a small town like Canadian. "I joke with my friends that living in Canadian is going to get me shot when I go back to Oklahoma City one day. We make eye contact here, we wave at everybody, we talk to everybody. I hadn't planned to stay, but now I think I will be here for a while."

On one condition, that is.

"As long as Laurie owns the paper."

CHAPTER NINE

They Don't Make 'Em Like That Anymore

In Billy Wilder's 1951 film *Ace in the Hole*, Kirk Douglas plays the part of a cocky, ambitious young reporter, Charles Tatum, who's been fired from a big city newspaper for slander, among other charges. When his car breaks down in Albuquerque (which qualified as the "sticks" back in the '50s), Tatum takes a job at the *Albuquerque Sun-Bulletin* and soon sees an opportunity to grab national headlines. A local cave-in at a mine suits his purposes to a tabloid t. This is the story, he figures, that will resurrect his career. By gaining "exclusive" access to the young miner trapped in the rubble, Tatum not only exploits his suffering but manipulates it, delaying the rescue operation in an effort to milk the story.

In other words, the "big-city" reporter is the bad guy. The good guy is the *Sun-Bulletin*'s editor, Jacob Q. Boot, a grizzled veteran who wears both a belt *and* suspenders as a symbol of journalistic caution, a reminder to always double-check the facts. A needlework sampler on the wall of his office reads, "Tell The Truth." But by the time Boot realizes that the hotshot reporter he has hired has absolutely no respect for that simple adage, the cave-in story has become a vehicle for Tatum's comeback, attracting national attention, hordes of spectators, and even a carnival that sets up outside the mine. Boot is outraged: "This is phony, below-the-belt journalism, that's what it is!"

Boot might be fictional, but he represents the almost mythical image of the small-town editor of American lore—someone who is compassionate, ethical, steeped in traditional values, and dedicated to truth over profit, even under threats of violence. And there are plenty of real-life examples to draw on, even though the descriptions of these esteemed pioneers often end with a sigh and some variation of the phrase, "they sure don't make 'em like that anymore."

But of course they do. Laurie Ezzell Brown and Ben Gish are typical of small-town editors who are carrying on a proud, and courageous, family tradition of speaking truth to power, often at considerable cost—personal, social, and economic. And M. E. Sprengelmeyer and Jason Miller are proof that newcomers are willing to take a gamble that people still care about community, connection, and—corny as it may sound—the truth.

But even as these editors are writing new chapters in the history of the weekly newspaper in America, it's important to remember the "Jacob Q. Boots" who laid the groundwork, journalists who displayed extraordinary courage in the face of almost insurmountable challenges. And by "challenges," I mean everything from death threats to arson, ad boycotts to social ostracism. Many of those face-offs took place in Appalachia and the South, especially in the 1950s and '60s, when coal companies wielded extraordinary power and the Ku Klux Klan waged a campaign of terror. Their decisions to take a stand, long before "advocacy journalism" became a catchphrase, came at considerable personal expense, of the kind that not all journalists would be willing to pay, then or now.

I am not sure, for example, how I would react if I was in the position of W. Horace Carter, editor of North Carolina's *Tabor City Tribune* in the 1950s—if my family received a number of death threats, or if I had found the following note under the windshield wiper of my car: "You are a nigger-loving son of a bitch. What you said about the Klan is all lies. We are honorable men and women who are interested in saving America from the Communists and Yankee liberals who are ruining the country. Stop writing those lies about us right now or you'll not wake up one morning."

Even though the Klan never made good on the threat against Carter's life, they did kill one of his dogs, just to drive home the point that they could get to his family at any time. Carter still continued to wage an editorial campaign against the KKK while the Klan maintained its campaign of violence toward blacks, Jews, and Catholics. Victims were abducted and flogged with bullwhips, and some had ears cut off. In a span of three years, Carter wrote more than one hundred Klan-related stories and editorials, a one-man outpouring of outrage. After one especially horrifying round of violence, Carter covered his front page with a headline printed in forty-eight-point bold type:

NIGHT-RIDING TERRORISTS BEAT
DISABLED VET, CRIPPLED FARMER
AND SICK, ELDERLY NEGRO WOMAN

You might think that a story about the Klan dragging innocent people from their homes in the dead of night, throwing them in the trunks of cars, driving them to remote spots, ripping off their clothes, and brutally flogging them would have had the citizenry up in arms. Not so. As Carter wrote in his autobiography, "Strangely, few people raised their voices to protest the terrorists. Not even the Pastor in the Tabor City Baptist Church, where I taught a Sunday School class, would publicly criticize the Klan floggings. Businessmen didn't want to alienate customers—and Klansmen were customers."

It's hard to imagine standing up to people who are threatening to kill you and your family when you are receiving no visible support from your friends and neighbors. But there must have been tacit support, because residents of Tabor City continued to buy the paper and merchants continued to advertise, despite threats from the Klan. And Carter's anti-Klan campaign did have several other, decidedly mixed, results: it brought the FBI to the region, and it led the North Carolina Klan's Grand Dragon, Tom Hamilton, to the newspaper office. Hamilton came in person to deliver the most terrifying threat of all, at least in Carter's mind: the threat of an advertising boycott. In his book, he recalls what he told Hamilton that day: "I can't last long without advertisers. I need every two-dollar subscriber I can find. But no amount of pressure you put on me will stop me from writing how I feel about the Klan as long as I have money to print another paper."

In the end, he outlasted them.

The public sentiment finally turned his way after dozens of Klansmen were convicted on charges ranging from kidnapping to assault. "Long reluctant to criticize the Klan movement," wrote Carter in his autobiography, "the people grasped the gravity of the court convictions and abandoned some of the fear as well as loyalty that had engulfed them during the Klan insurrection." He added, "I understood why they were unusually noncommittal. Throughout the rural areas and country villages, almost every resident was either a relative, close friend or neighbor of one or more Klansmen."

Perhaps Carter's most gratifying moment in his campaign

against the Klan came with the sentencing, on a single day in court, of some forty-nine Klansmen, including Tom Hamilton, who had by that time promoted himself to Imperial Wizard. The headline in the *Tribune* that week read, "Hamilton Gets 4-Year Term," and it was printed in the largest, blackest letters the printing foreman, J. A. Herlocker, could find. Carter remembers joking, "Really, J. A., I was saving that big type for the second coming of Jesus Christ, but in that you found it, let's run it."

It was to that point the biggest headline they had ever run. His paper pulled out that large type again only one other time, for the headline: "Tribune Wins Pulitzer." It shared the prize with another local paper, the *Whiteville News Reporter*. Never before had a weekly newspaper won a Pulitzer. The citation read: "For their successful campaign against the Ku Klux Klan, waged on their own doorstep at the risk of economic loss and personal danger, culminating in the conviction of over one hundred Klansmen and an end to terrorism in their communities." Carter was officially notified of the prize when a Western Union messenger brought him a telegram bearing the news. "It was ironic," remarked Carter, "that the local Western Union franchise was held by the late Troy Bennett, one of the Klansmen convicted for participating in the attacks."

Carter died in 2009, at the age of eighty-eight. But he continued to write and edit the paper until just before his death. His son says he often talked about the days of battling the Klan, and of having to move the family from place to place because of the threats. "He acknowledged being scared, especially for his family," his son told the *New York Times*. "But he was a newspaperman."

These days, when a *Wall Street Journal* list of the nation's 200 worst jobs can place "newspaper reporter" at 184 (well below "prison guard" and just above "stevedore"), it seems anachronistic for someone to claim that moniker with such pride. But not to Horace Carter, who put it this way in the closing pages of his book: "I say in all honesty that we did nothing any other conscientious newspaperman wouldn't have done if these hoodlum vigilantes were harassing and abusing his readers and neighbors, displaying disdain for law and order. I believe the simple word 'newspaperman' stands for justice, equality and freedom. And for that reason, and only that reason, I want my gravestone to be etched with that single word."

Horace Carter waged his editorial war against the North Carolina Klan in the early '50s. But the KKK would continue to carry on its campaign of hate and terror in the South for many more years. In the summer of 1964, a weekly paper called the *Neshoba Democrat* landed right in the middle of it.

It was known as Freedom Summer, and three young civil rights workers, all in their early twenties, had come to Philadelphia, Mississippi, to register black voters and to investigate the burning of a local church where their organizing efforts had been based. Anyone who has seen the film *Mississippi Burning* knows the basic story. The three young men—Michael Schwerner, James Chaney, and Andrew Goodman—were pulled over for speeding by a local law enforcement officer on June 21 and tossed in the Neshoba County jail. They were released late at night after paying a twenty dollar fine, and they were never seen alive again.

The editor of the *Neshoba Democrat* at the time, Jack Tannehill, did not have much sympathy for the three missing men, referring to them as "so-called civil rights workers" and "integrationists." In an editorial headlined "It's Time to Be Calm and Cool-headed," Tannehill wrote, "This is the first of many incidents, we have been told, that we will face this summer by outside agitators and demonstrators who say they are interested in voter registration in Mississippi."

On Tuesday, August 6, FBI agents discovered the bodies of the three young men buried in an earthen dam. By this time, the national press had arrived in Neshoba County and Tannehill's tone was consistently defensive. In editorials, he scolded the national media for depicting his community as "backward and ignorant."

Two years later, the *Neshoba Democrat* went from being defensive to taking the offensive, and in the pursuit of justice, not justification. This change owed to the work of the two editors who succeeded Tannehill. Over the years—more than forty years, in fact—Stanley Dearman and Jim Prince have refused to give up the fight to bring the killers to justice.

When Dearman bought the *Democrat*, he was well versed in the details of this case and frustrated by the evidence. He knew, for example, that seven men allied with the Ku Klux Klan had eventually been convicted on federal conspiracy charges in the case, but that none of them had served more than six years in prison. Eleven others went free. Even more appalling, he thought, was the fact that the state had never prosecuted a single person for the killings. He kept looking for ways to resurrect the story, to get the public to see the injustice in keeping silent.

In 1989, on the twenty-fifth anniversary of the killings, Dearman went to New York City to interview the mother of one of the slain men, Dr. Carolyn Goodman. That interview took up more than a full page of the newspaper and caught the attention of a young reporter in Alabama named Jim Prince, who still subscribed to the *Democrat*, his hometown paper. Prince wrote later that the interview "did more to change perceptions in Neshoba County than almost anything else. For the first time ever a human face was put on the civil rights workers, and over time, people—myself included, as a young man—began to accept Dearman's premise that murder is murder." The interview was a turning point for Prince, who left his job at a daily paper in Alabama and came home to Philadelphia, Mississippi, to work for Dearman and the *Democrat*.

In 2000, the crime still unresolved, Dearman urged the state attorney general to act in an editorial headlined, "It's Time For An Accounting."

There are those in this community who will say that it's been too long. The trouble with that position is that they were saying it after five years, after 10 years, after 15 years. If it involved a member of their family or a friend, they would never say it's been too long.

None of this would be an issue if a group of self-appointed saviors of the status quo had not taken it upon themselves to murder three unarmed young men who were arrested on a trumped-up charge and held in jail like caged animals until night fell and they could be intercepted by the Ku Klux Klan, a group whose bravery increases in direct proportion to their numbers and how long the sun has set.

The Klansmen may have thought they represented the community; they didn't represent everyone as, for example, the late Mrs. Annie Lee Welsh who, shortly after the murders, encountered an old man, obviously a Klan sympathizer, in front of a downtown shop. "Well, Lee," he said, "they did it for us." Miss Annie Lee drew up all of her five feet and 90 pounds into the man's face and said, between clenched teeth, "Well, they didn't do it for me."

This is a case that never goes away for the reason that it has never been dealt with in the way it should have been. It's time to bring a conclusion by applying the rule of law.

Come hell or high water, it's time for an accounting.

But as the fortieth anniversary of the killings neared, there was still no accounting. Dearman had sold the paper to Prince in 2000, and Prince picked up where his predecessor left off. In fact, the two men formed a coalition to mark the fortieth anniversary, adopting the motto, "Recognition, Resolution, Redemption: Uniting for Justice." Prince republished some of the *Democrat*'s stories about the murders from 1964, even though the articles revealed a more antagonistic racial tone from the paper's past.

Justice in the case finally came on June 21, 2005, when an eighty-year-year-old sawmill operator named Edgar Ray Killen was convicted on three counts of manslaughter. Even though the trial was televised, Prince wrote daily updates on the paper's Web site. He told the *American Journalism Review*: "We had a former mayor who said on the stand that the Klan was a good thing. People needed to know that. They needed to read about it in our paper." He added that the conviction "is finally lifting the cloud of fear from our community."

Dearman cried when he heard the verdict, which came forty-one years to the day, June 21, after the three young men disappeared.

For their courageous stand in the face of very real threats—both financial and physical—during their reporting about this case over the years, both editors and the *Neshoba Democrat* were recently honored with the Gish Award for courage, integrity, and tenacity in rural journalism. While awards are wonderful, of course, the true gifts come from the readers. Take this one, a post on the *Democrat*'s Web site following Killen's conviction: "I was six years old and living in Meridian when this crime occurred. My Aunt was very active with the Civil Rights and I as a child can remember the first Caucasian couple to visit my Grandmother's home. It was Mickey and Rita Schwerner, and it was less than two weeks later that Mickey, Andrew and James were reported missing. I cannot put into words the relief I felt when Mr. Killen was brought to justice."

In this digital age of nanosecond deadlines, when stories flash by with no apparent connection or context, such staying power—forty years on one story!—is astonishing. And yet, where else but a local paper, with an editor determined to outlast and outwit the bully *du jour*, would you find such determination? After all, they have to live there, too. Given the choice of either speaking up or moving out, exposing corruption or hunkering down, quite a few follow the tougher course of action. And only rarely does someone from the outside world take notice (and then, only in obituaries).

But not always.

Back in 1984, *Time* magazine singled out a number of newspapers—"Big Fish in Small Ponds," it called them—for their outstanding journalism. The article paid tribute to a couple of dailies with strong reputations for fighting corruption and civil rights violations—Virginia's *Fredericksburg Free-Lance Star* and Alabama's *Anniston Star*—but also took note of a small weekly (circulation 4,000) in the eastern Kentucky hamlet of Inez (population 500), the *Martin Countian*:

> The classic image of a weekly's editor is someone who writes much of the copy himself, shifting effortlessly from reporting

weddings, births and vacation trips to crusading against corruption. One lively example is Homer Marcum, 36, who in 1975 . . . launched his own weekly *Martin Countian*. . . . Marcum has clashed with the coal industry on environmental issues, and with the local Republican political machine, which, he alleges, buys votes in the guise of "assisting" people in the use of ballot machines. Since 1978 the *Martin Countian* has printed the name of every person who "assisted" a voter, and as a result, Marcum claims, the practice is diminishing.

That is the *Cliff Notes* version of Homer Marcum. According to Al Cross at the University of Kentucky's Institute for Rural Journalism and Community Issues, "Homer Marcum ran the gutsiest little paper in the county." In fact, he adds, "the *Martin Countian* was the best crusading newspaper in the United States in the 1980s. But he got sued, and it almost killed him."

He got sued by a local attorney named John Kirk, who owned and operated a rival newspaper, the *Martin Mercury*. The Kirk name is huge in eastern Kentucky, where many members of the family hold powerful political positions. The *Mercury*, which later became the *Martin County Times*, was not a publication known for challenging the status quo. As Marcum told *Time*, "Martin County is a good example of what can happen to a place when it receives no media attention. That is the breach I stepped into."

He stepped into a pile of trouble, too. He took on an entrenched political machine that had controlled the county for thirty years thanks in no small part to the Kirk family. The key elected position in eastern Kentucky had long been the county judge-executive, who controlled most of the state and federal tax money that flowed into the county. According to a 1982 article about the *Countian* in the *Harvard Crimson*, "Many county residents charge that past incumbents have completely sold-out to the coal companies." It goes on to note that this widespread corruption had led to political apathy, quoting one citizen as saying, "A lot of people here have been deprived and deceived so much by county officials and corporations, it's hard for them to trust anyone."

And certainly the political history of the area did not give them much comfort. Back in 1967, Judge-Executive Willie Kirk was convicted of embezzling federal funds and sentenced to twenty years in prison. But Kirk was pardoned by President Nixon after serving just five months of that sentence, and he went home to regain his post from his wife, who had held the position in his absence.

This was the environment that prompted Homer Marcum to become the voice of the voiceless, heralded by the *Countian's* slogan: "A Paper With Integrity" (which implied, of course, that the other paper in town had none). Marcum was teaching English and journalism to high school students in the county when he decided to start the paper. "I did it because of my mother, who was also a teacher in the county," he tells me. "She and other teachers had been asked to pay a kickback to county officials, in the form of buying 'tickets' to non-events. If they didn't buy these tickets, they were threatened with transfers to other schools."

He was outraged by the blatant corruption and was determined to expose it. And it wasn't hard, he tells me, because people would call with tips. "People just wanted their names kept out of it."

"Let me tell you a story," he says to me, during a conversation full of fascinating anecdotes that began just that way.

Vote buying was rampant, and those votes were bought any number of ways. One sure way was to promise to "fix" a person's driveway by using county-purchased gravel to make them a good driveway over what most often was a muddy car path.

The county court clerk, who wasn't a Kirk fan, called one day to say that she was certain that Willie Kirk had been selling the county's gravel to coal companies. She said she had personally seen eighteen-wheel coal trucks hauling gravel from the county's gravel pile. "You're the editor of the paper. I demand that you stop this waste of the taxpayer money. Just don't have my name on it," she said.

So I took my camera to the county garage and found the chain-link fence locked. But I could see that the gravel pile had been severely depleted. Knowing Willie and his record, I took a chance. I took a photo of the gravel pile, leaning against that chain-link fence. It wasn't a particularly good photo. I always believed the best photos were ones with people in them. This was only of a gravel pile.

In the next paper, I printed that photo above the fold on the front page and wrote a simple cut line that read something like this:

"This is the county's gravel pile. Judge Willie Kirk has been giving gravel away. You should call Willie to make sure you get your share of the gravel for your own road before it is all gone. Here is his office number . . . and here is his home telephone number. . . ." It was unlisted, but I knew the number.

Some of my former journalism students worked in Willie's office and I called one and asked her to let me know what the reaction would be the next day when the paper came out.

Early the next morning, just hours after the paper was on the street, I got a call from a lady whose voice sounded feeble. "Mr. Marcum, I called Willie Kirk's office just like you said to do in the paper. The road is impassable and I need gravel in the worst way. I can't even get my car out to go to the store or to the doctor. I talked to Willie and he was furious at you. He said he couldn't give me any gravel because you would take a picture of it and put it in the paper and he would wind up in big trouble. Willie said I should call you. He said if you would promise not to take his picture, he would bring me some gravel and put it on my driveway. So my question, Mr. Marcum, is this: Will you not take a picture if Willie brings me some gravel?"

I told her that she should tell Willie that I would agree not to take his picture this one time, but only this one time, that she should be able to have gravel for her driveway.

Back in Willie's office, my mole told me that Willie was outraged. The phone had been ringing off the hook and that Willie kept telling people to quit calling him about gravel.

That stopped the gravel giveaways. That was the one time that Willie might have had a cause of action against me in court *if* I had been incorrect about his gravel shenanigans. I never heard a word from Willie about it.

Anticipating a question about the ethics of this approach, Marcum adds, "I know that's unconventional journalism. But I was between a rock and a hard place. They'd declared war against me for telling the truth. I declared war on them by vowing to tell the *whole* truth about their actions."

And his crusade to tell the whole truth paid off. People responded to his stories by voting out those politicians whose "shenanigans" he had exposed. Even so, the political machine was not about to give up. Just days after an election in which Willie Kirk had been ousted as county judge-executive, only a month before he would have to surrender his office, Marcum got tipped to a secret meeting that was about to be held at the courthouse. "So I went there," he tells me, "and Kirk and his magistrates were about to hold a meeting. I called them on it, saying 'What the hell are you guys doing?'"

He points out that he had not received a public notification as required under the Sunshine Law. The attendees were trying to pass a couple of motions without advertising them to the public, another illegal act. Both motions involved a parcel of land connected to a housing project that had been built with federal funding. (There were Kirks in many government offices, including the housing agency, which built this project with federal dollars.) The parcel in question was swampland. The first motion would have labeled this land "surplus," which would have allowed Kirk's nephew to buy it for one dollar. The second motion called for a bond measure of one million dollars to build a supermarket on that land.

A lawyer reluctantly handed over the motions and Marcum had a chance to read them. He told those at the meeting, "'You assholes can't do this without a public hearing.'" Marcum and *his* lawyer went to court the next day and got an injunction against those motions, citing a violation of the Sunshine Law. He won that round, but the Kirks never let up.

Marcum's relentless exposure of scandal—from strip mining violations to tax fraud—came at a cost. The *Countian* was sued seven times by John Kirk, who was a lawyer, after all. Marcum won every single time, but defending against the lawsuits was expensive, not to mention wearying. The battle took a financial, psychological, and sometimes even physical toll; Marcum was occasionally punched by people he wrote about. "In 1989," says Marcum, "I was nearly at the end of my rope."

What prompted Marcum to finally sell the paper, says Al Cross, "was meeting a woman from Tennessee on a ski vacation." That woman became his wife, and they decided to make their home in Tennessee. But Marcum did not want to leave town without making sure that a free press would survive in Martin County.

"John Kirk and I still weren't speaking," Marcum explains, but the *Countian* editor thought he had some leverage. He had heard that Kirk was lying about his circulation numbers in an effort to wrest the legal advertising away from the *Martin Countian*. "In coal country," Marcum notes, "a notice of 'intention to mine' is a common legal ad, and those legal ads were worth 10 percent of the *Countian*'s profits." And the legal ads went to the paper with the highest circulation.

Marcum says he sent his lawyer over to make Kirk an offer: he would keep quiet about Kirk's circulation chicanery if Kirk would sell Marcum his newspaper for a dollar; he would then promise to turn around and sell his own paper to a third party, a newspaper chain with a reputation for independent journalism. "I wanted to insulate the paper from politics," says Marcum. "I couldn't walk away otherwise."

I called John Kirk for his version of this transaction, and, not surprisingly, it differs sharply. "That's not accurate," states Kirk, who still practices law in Martin County. "I have a vague, distant memory of Homer saying something like that" (about the circulation figures), "but I just thought it would be a good idea and a good time to sell." He expressed surprise that Marcum would characterize their relationship as contentious, even though he conceded that there had been a number of lawsuits between them. "I thought Homer Marcum and I were friends," he says. "He's spun this story a different way. And that's the truth of it." The truth of it, at least the truth they both agree on, is that Kirk and Marcum agreed to sell their papers to a third party.

Today, Marcum is communications director for a children's

health care facility in Greeneville, Tennessee, where he lives with his wife, a cardiac nurse. Soon after he sold the paper, he was asked to speak to the Tennessee Press Association about his crusading career at the *Countian*. "It was the first time I'd talked about it since leaving," he says. "I couldn't get through the speech. I broke down and cried. I mean, how do you sell your baby? It's not easy. Everyday, I think, 'I'll bet they're doing the same old shit back home.'" He swears he will not go back, but he did end our conversation by pointing out that, after five bypass surgeries, "Now I can run sprints. I'm in the same shape I was back when I was fighting Willie Kirk."

In hopes that young journalists will take up where he left off, Marcum speaks to college journalism classes on a regular basis. His message to them is a combination of the philosophical and the prosaic: "It's absolutely God's work," he says, "to make sure taxes are spent wisely."

Homer Marcum, Kentucky muckraker, sounds like a character right out of an Elmore Leonard novel. In fact, a lot of these legendary editors would make great material for films or television shows. But the work of the small-town editor is usually not so much dramatic as it is downright delightful. And no one describes the delightful detail of small-town life better than country editor Henry Beetle Hough. Almost a century later, his tale of giving up big-city journalism for the life of a weekly editor is inspirational and timeless.

When Henry and Betty Hough moved to Martha's Vineyard to become editors and publishers of the *Vineyard Gazette* in 1920, they were newly wed, but not new to journalism. They had met at the Columbia School of Journalism and started their careers in New York City. In his classic book about small-town newspapering, *Country Editor*, Henry Beetle Hough discusses their decision to leave the big city behind, move to a (then) remote island, and take over a paper with a circulation of 600.

"We were young, and we liked the smell of the old office upstairs over the grocery store. One year, I worked in New York for a corporation with gross sales of almost a million dollars a day. The *Gazette* was everything which that was not."

Anyone hoping to understand what that "everything" means—all the charms and challenges of telling the so-called small stories in "small" places—would be well served by starting with this incredible book. I treasure my copy, which is signed by Walter Cronkite, who wrote the introduction to the anniversary edition. As he recalled,

> The book came out in 1940. That was a busy year for those of us in our early twenties who proudly counted ourselves as "newspapermen." The war raged in Europe, our engagement seemed likely and many of us working for big city newspapers or wire services were beginning to jockey for the opportunity to report from overseas.
>
> And then Henry Hough's book hit the stores. I remember reading it with eye-popping, brain-grabbing absorption. Here was a lyrical description of the small-town life of a *weekly* newspaper publisher. It was a revelation.
>
> I almost physically felt myself skidding to a stop on my career path—the one leading to success in metropolitan journalism. Suddenly I found myself considering an option that Henry Hough had opened for me.

Cronkite obviously did not drop his career path to head for the sticks, although he would spend many happy years on Martha's Vineyard and many delightful moments in the company of the Houghs. But he realized that this book was the first of its kind, a beguiling beacon to journalists looking to tell universal stories through the narrow lens of life in a small town. The masthead of the *Gazette* proudly touted the island's small size and insularity over the years. By 1985, the year Henry Hough died, it read: "Island of Martha's Vineyard, seven miles off southeast coast of Massachusetts. Winter population: 12,000; in summer, 62,000. Twenty miles from city of New Bedford, 80 miles from Boston and 150 miles from New York."

Of course, when the Houghs first started publishing the *Gazette*, the population was much smaller and the feeling of isolation more severe. In order to engage their new neighbors, they enlisted the help of local "correspondents" around the island to write up dispatches about their communities each week. His description of one of these locals, seventy-year-old Dora Trapp Carrington, is especially vivid:

"For many years, she had been writing her items in precise and altogether beautiful script in blue ink, usually on scraps of linen paper, and she had no notion of retiring. There was something encouraging about her envelope turning up every Wednesday, her penmanship never faltering, never deviating so much as a hair. It seemed to suggest that Mrs. Carrington was always on the job, always the chronicler of the social life of her town, no matter what crises might arise."

Mrs. Carrington, we are told, was a proud descendant of the island's original settlers, who reached shore in 1642. As Hough put it, "She was real, real as the boulders in the pastures of her ancestral home, and just about as rugged. But her ruggedness was well-cloaked in gentility."

Mrs. Carrington had a unique style, wrote Hough, that might best be described as "mellifluous": "We groaned a little at first because to her, no one ever died, but everyone passed away.

She was not above saying that a prominent citizen had 'passed from the earth life to the heavenly.' If she wanted to speak of *solariums* instead of *sunparlors*, she usually did so in a way which made *solarium* seem natural (except, sometimes, to the surprised owner of the house). She reported 'noble and eloquent' addresses which received 'rapturous applause.'" To think of Mrs. Carrington, Hough concluded, "was to think of the rustle of a silken gown."

He loved the idiom of the country paper, the elaborations that make the most mundane events come alive. "The city press is poorer," he said, "because it is so bare, so hard, so sharp, so fast. . . . Often is it more difficult to write easily of the homely, intimate things than it is to write of battles and conflagrations and Arctic explorations."

As an example, he pointed to the difficulty of writing articles about club meetings. The standard "lead" simply did not exist for such a story: "There was no *news* in the city sense of the word. The main thing was that the meeting was held—a fact of some interest to the members—and we thought the best way to do this was to say that the meeting was held, as simply and directly as possible, and then to go on with the subject of the meeting and the refreshments."

But that one item—the refreshments—turned into quite a kerfuffle. The paper's practice of describing the refreshments served at all these meetings kindled a lot of jealousy. "We kept getting complaints," said Hough, "that the whipped cream had been omitted from the fruit salad cup in the Ladies' Social Circle report, or that the *Gazette* had seemed to favor the patty shells of the Degree of Pocahontas over the lettuce sandwiches of the Occidental Chapter, Daughters of Plutarch."

After awhile, the *Gazette* made an office rule that all

refreshments would be described as "delicious," no more or less. But the writers grew weary of the word "delicious" and finally the policy was changed; reporters were to say only that "refreshments were served. We do not characterize them. They must stand on their own feet."

In addition to the more mundane events reported in the *Gazette*, now and then a story came along that actually made headlines in the mainstream, mainland press. The murder of Martin Willis, to name one. Willis was a hard-drinking local resident who was also one of the *Gazette*'s "correspondents." He dropped off his copy at the newspaper office on a fateful Thursday, the day the staff put together the paper for Friday's publication. Late in the day, they received a phone message that Willis had been shot and killed by another local resident, Norman Strowd. No one knew the details, but they scrambled to get as much information as they could before "putting the paper to bed."

It was only the third murder on the island in three hundred years, so it obviously made news off-island as well. Before long, wrote Hough, residents could hear the drone of engines from airplanes bringing in mainland reporters. Hough ran into a carload of them.

"They were in high spirits, as if on some kind of lark. I knew that Stroud was at the jail, but I sent them off to the State Police barracks, six or eight miles away, because I did not like the way they talked, and judged the ride would be good for them. Anyway, I wanted them out of town."

As this big story was coming together in the *Gazette* office, Hough wrote, "there was a disturbance in the street in front of the office. A cat belonging in the house across the way had been struck and killed by a hit-and-run driver. We saw Gus

Peters pick up the bleeding, dead animal and carry it tenderly into his yard. The cat's name was Skippy. We set an obituary for Skippy, together with some remarks concerning drivers who hit pet animals and do not even stop to see what they have done."

In a matter of hours, the *Gazette* managed to get out the paper with more details of the murder of Martin Willis, including the observations of an eyewitness to the shooting, than any of the big-city reporters had managed to gather.

> "When we took the papers to the post office," wrote Hough, one of the clerks said to me, "What a shame that was! Things like that are terrible."
>
> "Yes," I said.
>
> "Did they find out who did it?" he asked.
>
> "Find out who did what?"
>
> "Who killed Gus' cat," he said.

That anecdote pretty much sums up the difference between city and country journalism. The small stuff matters.

At Henry Hough's funeral in 1985, the minister talked about that legacy of storytelling:

> Thoreau once said that one is not born into the world to do everything but to do something. Henry Hough did something for 65 years—with a small newspaper, in a small town, on a small island. And he did it with such a deliberate and concentrated attention that the world off-Island soon took notice.
>
> What he wrote and what he stood for was so specific to this place that it was universal.

Reading about Henry Hough got me thinking about M. E. Sprengelmeyer, another big-city reporter who came to a small town to weave universal stories out of the daily dramas of everyday life. And, like Hough, everyday life in a small town is teaching him more than he ever dreamed.

In the February 4th issue of the *Guadeloupe County Communicator*, Sprengelmeyer wrote about his harrowing drive through a treacherous snowstorm to pick up the printed copies of the paper from Clovis, New Mexico, a three-hour drive.

> The printer's loading dock was blocked by snow drifts. I circled the block and got stuck on a snow-packed side street. As a brave friend from the printing plant helped me dig out the tires, for a few seconds I wondered if I should surrender to Mother Nature, hunker down in Clovis overnight and make the 99-mile drive back to Santa Rosa some other day.
>
> No way.
>
> People count on their newspaper. I thought about the steady stream of people who show up at our offices each Thursday to get the edition hot off the presses. I thought about the advertisers expecting their precious coupons to be on the streets for a full seven days. I thought about my neighbor who'd need something to read while snowed-in at her house. If nothing else, people would need the kindling for their wood stoves.

> This week marks my six month anniversary as publisher of *The Communicator*, and I'm only now coming to grips with the big-time responsibility that comes with running a newspaper.
>
> Six months into the adventure, I've had more white-knuckle moments than that drive during last week's snow storm. But I'll also tell you what I tell my friends back in D.C. when they ask.
>
> I'm having far more fun than I ever imagined.

Since I am now a regular subscriber to the *Guadalupe County Communicator* (among other weeklies I have collected on this journey), I find myself wondering about the fate of that water slide and the progress of the come-from-behind high school football team. I am also occasionally surprised by something that crops up on its front page. A profile of Miguel Marquez, for example, told me something I had never known before. Marquez, a reporter who worked in the ABC News Los Angeles Bureau at the same time I did, is a native of Santa Rosa. "When he was younger," wrote Sprengelmeyer, "his family ran the Square Deal store downtown and he attended local schools." Marquez is now based in London. He still tries to visit New Mexico as often as he can, Sprengelmeyer noted. "But his latest trip, which was supposed to be a two-week stay, was cut short when he was called back to Europe to cover the earthquakes in Italy. Such is the reporter's life."

There is a circular feeling to this, I realize. A local kid makes good as a foreign correspondent, and his story is written by a foreign correspondent who is now making good as the local publisher. And it's being read by a former correspondent who used to work with one of them and is now writing a book about the other.

But I really experienced a coming-full-circle moment the day I spotted a front-page photo of author Rudolfo Anaya dedicating an elementary school in Albuquerque named in his honor. Anaya, I learned from the article, was a native of Guadalupe County. A related article informed me that Hollywood producers had come to Santa Rosa to scout for potential locations for a film adaptation of Anaya's book *Bless Me, Ultima*. This was the same book, you may recall, that prompted such an uproar in my town of Norwood, Colorado, and compelled the *Norwood Post* to spring into action on behalf of the First Amendment.

Like any journalist in search of perfect transitions, I can spot a God-given segue when I see one.

Time to go home again, I thought.

CHAPTER TEN

Coming Home

Since I first started on this journey down journalism's blue highways, my own hometown newspaper, the *Norwood Post*, has gone through some radical changes.

The editor who took over after the *Bless Me Ultima* flap, Bob Beer, lived in Telluride and commuted down-valley to Norwood to edit and do reporting for the paper. He left a previous job as reporter for a Telluride paper because he needed a break from the intense political atmosphere in that upscale resort. "I liked the smaller stuff," he said, "and I was tired of the Type A Telluride types." When the *Norwood Post* position opened up, he jumped at it and found a different atmosphere: "Politics is below the surface in Norwood. I don't go around kicking cow pies looking for worms."

Beer operated as a one-man band. He worked in the cramped, dusty office of the *Post*—just across the street from the Lone Cone Saloon, and around the corner from the Splish Splash Buggy Bath—surrounded by piles of old issues and a wall of plaques touting years and years of journalism awards (a ubiquitous décor for small- town weeklies and a testament to the generosity of state press associations). He would have loved to hire a reporter or two to help him out, he remarked, but the *Post* was owned by Gateway Press, a Midwestern newspaper chain that was more interested in profiting from local advertising than improving the editorial content.

"On the positive side," said Beer, "no one is looking over my shoulder." On the negative side, no one was looking over his copy, either, which led to a few early glitches when he misspelled the names of local residents or, worse, misidentified them. Names, lots of them, are the most valuable currency of the small- town paper. Getting them wrong is editorial suicide. And he once got the vote count wrong for a school board election, which made people so angry he featured a photo of himself wearing a dunce cap in the next issue, by way of apology.

But that was about as controversial as it got. Certainly, one look at the *Norwood Post* in those days told you that hard-hitting investigative journalism was not its forte. One front-page photo featured a turkey buzzard perched on a fence, looking out at a mown hay field. I actually thought it was a terrific picture—artfully framed, the fading autumn light on the shorn field portending the coming winter, the enormous bird serving as a sentry to seasonal change. I told Beer I admired it and asked him if he had intended to make a visual and poetic statement.

"I intended to make my deadline. I had nothing and I had to go to press. Saw that buzzard, got out of the car, and snapped the picture." In broadcasting, we call that "making air, not art." Now and then, of course, you luck out and make both.

Beer soon discovered that living in Telluride was not the best way to find out what was really going on in Norwood. "I missed the late-night talk at the Lone Cone Saloon," he said, "and that's really where you find out what folks are talking about." He also worried about ad revenue. The Telluride papers were competing for the same business.

His fears were prescient. Another publishing group, 13th Street Media, bought the *Norwood Post* in 2008. The owner lives in Boulder, Colorado. But this was, at least, a "chain" of only three small papers—the *Telluride Daily Planet*, the *Explorer* in Tucson, and the *Norwood Post*. And the publisher, Andrew Mirrington, also lives nearby, in Telluride. According to conventional wisdom, local publishers have less of a "bean-counting" mentality and more concern for the editorial side of the business.

The debate over the future of small- town papers usually turns on a rather simplistic question: "Which is better, family-owned or chain-owned?" Benjy Hamm, the editorial director at Landmark Community Newspapers, a chain of fifty-six newspapers, has experienced both sides of the equation. He started at a small family-owned paper in North Carolina and bought into the idea that a local owner would more likely stand up to pressure from local politicians and advertisers.

"So my early belief," he tells me, "was family-owned was the best, no comparison. I've changed my view. Both sides can have lousy newspapers. It's not the ownership. It's the commitment."

"If you have a local [family] owner with deep pockets [to fight libel suits] and good ethics, then you're okay," he says. But having a big company behind you sometimes helps. "When local people want to threaten a local paper with ad boycotts, and they realize the paper is part of a bigger corporation, it might give them more pause."

Hamm says his company never interferes with editorial policy at their newspapers, even though he wishes some of them were better: "I can't make them cover city council meetings." But he is ready to help with legal and editorial advice if asked. "If you have a tough story you're working on, I can be an editor at a distance."

Distance has a downside, he adds. There is sometimes more turnover in the top editorial jobs at a chain-owned paper, whereas a local owner and publisher lives in a town and plans to stay. "There can be a loss of continuity in understanding the community."

Andrew Mirrington, now the publisher of both the *Norwood Post* and the *Telluride Daily Planet*, saw that the *Post* was struggling to find enough local businesses to buy ads to support the paper. By making the *Post* an eight-page wrap-around (rather than an insert) to the *Planet*, says Mirrington, "we've been able to move about 750 papers each week in Norwood," where the in- town population is just 500 people.

He also insisted on hiring an editor who lived in town. Ellen Metrick, a former school teacher who moved to Norwood with her husband, an agent with the National Resources Conservation Service, jumped at the chance to be editor even though it pays little and is something of an "adjunct" position. "Somehow the paper validates the town and our very existence," Metrick comments. "It says, 'We are here, in print, there is something physical.' We can say, 'Look, we won the game, we have this great art teacher!'"

She understands why the company had to cut back on the number of pages. "The *Norwood Post* can probably not stand alone in terms of ads," she says. Despite the relatively large number of restaurants in town (five), the only one that can afford to advertise is the Happy Belly Deli, and that's only because it gives Metrick free lunches when she conducts interviews there.

So she understands why the *Post* has become the "pita bread" for the more substantial filling provided by the *Planet*. Even so, she was unhappy when Mirrington made the decision to shut down the *Post*'s office to save money and told Metrick to work from home. "People thought we went away," she says, "they thought we'd disappeared." They can't walk in the door and visit like they used to—often a valuable source of information. Norwoodians, it seems, are decidedly *not* "on-the-record" types. When Metrick tried to get quotes from locals about hopes for the New Year, she had trouble getting permission to use names, even for this innocuous subject.

"'2010? Bring it on, I'm ready for it, whatever it is!' said one person, who wished to remain anonymous. She added, 'The worst part of 2009 was the unexpected surprises . . . but those also often turned out to be the best parts.'"

Metrick says she is still working to gain the trust of local residents, even though she is one herself. And while she covers the usual local government meetings, she is focusing more on school news. "The school is the hub of this community," she states, and news about the kids' achievements—athletic, artistic, and academic—is guaranteed to sell papers. And she's gone even further with the idea, starting a "youth page" in which students write some of the articles each week. And once a month, the students write a four-page newspaper that gets printed as an insert. With a grant from the Telluride Foundation, the students were able to get some production software for school computers. "If the kids know how to use this," she says, "they can get jobs anywhere that printing is a required skill." Like a newspaper, perhaps.

She's going to need all *her* skills in the coming months. A major story is developing in the area, one that has already attracted attention from the mainstream media. The issue: the controversial proposal by the Toronto-based Energy Fuels

Corporation to build the Pinon Ridge uranium mill in Paradox Valley (not far from Norwood, Nucla, and Naturita). It would be the nation's first uranium mill built in nearly three decades and reflects the country's renewed interest in nuclear energy.

"When running at full capacity," wrote the *Telluride Watch*, "the mill would use 300 gallons of water per minute to process 21 truckloads per day containing 500 tons of uranium ore into yellow cake uranium and processed vanadium, seven days a week, 350 days a year, for an operating life of 40 years. The uranium would eventually go to nuclear power plants and the vanadium would be used to strengthen steel."

The Montrose County commissioners voted in the fall of 2009 to approve a special-use permit for the facility to be sited on 880 acres now zoned for agricultural use in Paradox Valley. If you have seen the movie *Thelma and Louise*, you might recognize this vista: a long, narrow ribbon of a highway running through a magnificent valley, with sheer, red rock cliffs on either side. Our family loves to hike in the area, searching out the ancient Indian petroglyphs hidden among the rocks. It's called "Paradox" because the river does not run the length of the valley, as most rivers do, but straight across it. It's home to cattle ranches, farms, and a quaint little general store that marks the "town" of Bedrock.

It is also home to the Uravan Mineral Belt, a formation that contains one of the country's largest concentrations of high-grade uranium and vanadium.

As you might imagine, the proposal is highly contentious. A couple of environmental groups have filed suits to block the application, while many people who live in the West Valley are fighting to get the mill approved. Many of them come from old mining families and remember the "boom" times of the past when uranium mining was big business here. Energy Fuels has said the mill would provide 85 new jobs with average salaries of $40 to $75 thousand a year as well as 200 ancillary jobs.

In the nearby communities of Uravan, Nucla, Naturita, Egnar, and Dove Creek, where trailers are a common form of housing, just as many stores are shuttered as they are open, and people are desperate for work, there is not really a question: the mine would be a blessing.

Proponents stated their position loud and clear (emphasis on loud) at a number of hearings held in the county. As one advocate was quoted in the *Telluride Daily Planet*, residents had to ask themselves "'which is more important, the birds that live in the trees or the families who live on the ground?'"

Equally vocal opponents (including Telluride celebrities like Darryl Hannah) are worried about the impact of radioactive waste and dust on health and the environment as well as agriculture and recreation in Paradox Valley. A story in the June 17, 2009, edition of the *Norwood Post* by editor Deb Dion (who preceded Metrick) framed opposition to the mill proposal around the concerns of a woman who farms in the valley.

> Marie Moore just picked the season's first cherries from her tree, on her small family orchard in Paradox Valley. Some of the young trees are producing fruit for the first time, as this rainy spring has made the valley especially lush and verdant.
>
> Usually, says Moore, this would make her happy—but she can't shake the feeling of dread she has about contamination from the proposed uranium near her land.

It is extremely unlikely that you would ever read that lead in a story appearing in the *San Miguel Basin Forum*, the weekly paper serving those poorer communities in the west end of

Montrose County. In response to opponents who like to point out that the new mill would be located just 12 miles from the area's last remaining uranium mill, a plant in Uravan that was dismantled during a $120-million, 20-year EPA Superfund cleanup, the *Forum* quotes local supporters like Cindy Carrothers: "My Mom and her family swam the Union Carbide pool in Uravan in the late 1950's and they don't glow in the dark. My Mother had five children and we are all well. None of us has two heads or five arms."

That sentiment is echoed in the letters to the editor:

It never ceases to amaze me how many times the green beans from Telluride, Moab, Norwood and, yes, Paradox, are there against the mill because of the harmful dust, chemicals that are trucked in, radiation that will "harm their tomatoes." The questions they ask Energy Fuels over and over and over again have already been answered many, many times by experts. . . . I personally feel that the people from Telluride, Norwood and Moab should stay home and take care of their own back yards. All of the "harmful gases" from all the ski buses, the traffic, cutting big slices out of the mountains for ski runs, the tourists who trash hotel rooms and sheets. Then they wouldn't have to go around to other towns with their signs: "Radiation Kills." Radiation also heals.

In case you hadn't picked up on it, this issue splits down socioeconomic fault lines. And those living in hardscrabble conditions in the West End don't think the celebrities and "green beans" of Telluride, who spend maybe a month out of the year in their second homes, have a clue about what those jobs will mean to the poorer communities.

That may be true. But it is also true that "facts" tend to be slippery creatures at these public hearings, and the scientific facts about modern uranium mining are likely to be spun 'round and 'round like so much (radioactive) dust in the wind before this thing is settled. In January 2011, state regulators approved a license for the mill to be built. But the plan still faces challenges over transportation and emissions permits, and opponents have vowed to keep fighting.

The *Norwood Post* is positioned right in the middle, both geographically and culturally. "I've had miners tell me, 'Yeah, we die from complications of uranium mining, but that's the way life is,'" says Metrick. "And a woman in Nucla claims her whole family is healthy even though they grew up playing on the tailings pile at the Superfund site." But she also hears from farmers and ranchers in Paradox Valley who "worry that no one will want to buy their crops or beef because of the radioactive dust and pollution." And then there are all those folks who are just antinuclear no matter what form it takes.

This story, as they say, has legs. And Metrick plans to run with it. "I'd really like to do this for a while," she says. As she starts experiencing that "too close for comfort" syndrome, when her attempts at fairness make her a target of both sides in the debate, she might take heart knowing that stories about mining and its hazards first appeared in what was then the *Norwood Star* some fifty years ago. I know this because a friend in Norwood presented me with some very dirty, yellowed old copies he found in a structure he was renovating. "MILL TO SHUT DOWN!" shouted one headline. But even as I searched through these weathered, decades-old copies of the paper, I found myself drawn not to the stories about the uranium boom and bust but to the smaller triumphs and tragedies of everyday life.

One article bemoaned the fact that the Norwood school grounds "are without even a lawn, trees or shrubbery. We think it is high time that the members of our school board bury the hatchet on this question and take interest in the school property." A column by a local farmer read, "Loren came tearing into the house to report that there was a hawk in the chicken house and that it had killed a lot of the chickens. The hawk turned out to be a large owl that we had heard hooting back up the creek for several nights. The chickens, panicked by its diving at them, sought refuge in the corners. The dead ones, nine in all, died from suffocation rather than from injuries inflicted by the owl. The owl population was soon decreased by one." Not a major crime spree, obviously, but the story still has its twists and turns.

And speaking of twists and turns, a story headlined "Mrs. Frank Belisle and Two Daughters Killed in Accident" in the November 23, 1950, edition of the *Norwood Star* is a vivid reminder that life in the mountains has always been treacherous:

> For the second time this year, a motor vehicle accident on Norwood Hill has claimed the lives of three persons. The latest victims are Mrs. Frank Belisle, 24, and her two small daughters, Sharon Ann, 3, and Linda Jean, 8 months. The trio left their home in Fruitvale Wednesday to go to Norwood to help the children's grandparents, Mr. and Mrs. James Belisle, celebrate their 50th wedding anniversary—but they never arrived.
>
> Alarmed at their failure to appear, D. J. Royer, a cousin of Frank Belisle, began a yard by yard scrutiny of Norwood Hill. . . . About one half mile down the roadway from the top of the hill, Royer noted marks that resembled those of a motor vehicle wheel. Checking the precipitous slope, he first found

a child's toy and then three hundred feet from the roadway he came upon the lifeless body of little Linda. Mrs. Belisle was another 100 feet down the canyonside and 18 yards farther down the slope was Sharon Ann lying near the body of the family pet, a cocker spaniel.

A separate article, "James Belisle Dies of Heart Attack," makes no reference to the first one and was apparently added at the last moment. It reads, "Jim Belisle, one of the old time residents of San Miguel County, died Wednesday night at his home in Norwood of a heart attack. Mr. Belisle, who had not been ill, was sitting on the davenport when he was stricken. A complete obituary will be printed next week."

Every time I drive up the mile-long tortuous terror known as Norwood Hill (especially in winter), trying not to look over the sharp drop-off to the San Miguel River below, I think of the accidents along this stretch. It's hard *not* to think about them, actually, because of the crosses that have been erected by the side of the road. These crosses have even more of an impact on those who know the stories behind them. And they know the stories because they have a newspaper. *Their* newspaper.

"One measure of whether people are connected in a community," says Al Cross of the Institute for Rural Journalism and Community Issues, "is whether they say 'my paper' or 'our paper.' They never say 'THE paper.'"

My paper—the *Norwood Post*—is hanging on by its news-nails right now, but only because the town, and the usual advertisers, are feeling the pain of the economic downturn. Elsewhere in the country, the weekly newspaper is not just surviving but thriving. An inaugural survey of small and medium newspapers by two trade groups—the Suburban Newspapers of America

(SNA) and the National Newspaper Association—found that while sales for the newspaper industry as a whole were down by as much as 15 percent in 2008 (probably more by now), revenues for papers with circulations of under 100,000 fell an average of only 2 percent. "Community papers are affected by the current economic downturn, but they are not in a crisis," said SNA president Nancy Lane. "In fact, there are some that are showing growth."

But more important than the "business model," at least as far the readers are concerned, is the twin payoff of connectivity and continuity. As I witnessed when Jason Miller resurrected the *Concrete Herald*, people in the community can become downright emotional about their local newspaper. Without a paper, *their* paper, they feel disconnected from their neighbors. With a paper, they have a sense of their collective history, a continuity of shared experiences. As Ellen Metrick put it, "The paper says 'we are here.'"

So the audience is not going anywhere. As for replacing the older journalists when they get weary of the weekly grind, Benjy Hamm says the mainstream media's loss may be the weekly's gain. He is seeing more and more résumés from eager, young editors and big-city journalists who have either been victims of "downsizing" or grown weary of wondering if they are next. "If you think in terms of where [there] are the opportunities to be [a] top editor of a paper, there are eight thousand opportunities at smaller papers."

I had so many of those papers on my "try-to-get-there" list, and I regret not visiting more. So many friends would hear about this project and say, "Well, you've *got* to go to my hometown and visit the [fill-in-the-blank]—it's a terrific little paper!" And so my list includes names like the *Moosehead Messenger*, the

Berkshire Eagle, and the *Pocahontas Times*, to name just a few. Or the *Freeman's Journal* in Cooperstown, New York, whose owner and editor, Jim Kevlin, waxed eloquent in the *American Journalism Review* about his decision to leave the world of big-city daily editing for what he calls "liberation journalism."

"Foremost," writes Kevlin, "this is pure journalism. You can cover what you want the way you think it should be covered. You can free yourself from the corrosive union that's developed between journalism and marketing—two warring animals—in the past quarter-century. To the degree you can tolerate the consequences, you can speak truth to power."

"To the degree you can tolerate the consequences," of course, is just another way of saying "you have to live there, too."

Or rather, you *get* to live there, too.

And for those who wonder why anyone would live in a small town, where stories can range from club news to Klan news, from broken treaties to broken hearts, from banned books to escaped emus, I leave you with the words of Henry Beetle Hough, the "country editor" of Martha's Vineyard:

"At first, there were visitors who asked, 'What are you doing in a one-horse town like this?' I did not know what to answer. It was not a matter which could be explained with any chance of success to the sort of person who would ask the question."

BIBLIOGRAPHY

Published Sources

Anderson, Bruce. *The Mendocino Papers*. Vol. 1. Boonville CA: Bruce Anderson, 2008.

Adams, Charles C. *Boontling, An American Lingo: With a Dictionary of Boontling*. Philo CA: Mountain House Press, 1990.

Carter, Horace C. *Only in America: An Autobiography of a Weekly Newspaperman and Business Success*. Tabor City NC: Atlantic Publishing, 2001.

Hough, Henry Beetle. *Country Editor*. 2nd ed. West Dennis MA: The Peninsula Press, 1997.

Lauterer, Jock. *Community Journalism: Relentlessly Local*. 3rd ed. Chapel Hill: University of North Carolina Press, 2006.

Lende, Heather. *If You Lived Here, I'd Know Your Name: News from Small-town Alaska*. Chapel Hill NC: Algonquin Books, 2005.

Look, Al. *Unforgettable Characters of Western Colorado*. Boulder CO: Pruett Press, 1966.

Pumarlo, Jim. *Bad News and Good Judgment: A Guide to Reporting on Sensitive Issues in a Small-town Newspaper*. Oak Park IL: Marion Street Press, 2005.

Stiles, Jim. *Brave New West: Morphing Moab at the Speed of Greed*. Tucson: University of Arizona Press, 2007.

Other Media

FILM

Brave New West. Directed by Doug Hawes-Davis and Drury Gunn Carr. Missoula MT: High Plains Films, 2008.

NEWSPAPERS

Anderson Valley Advertiser,
   Boonville, California
Apsáalooke Nation,
   Crow Agency, Montana
Big Horn County News,
   Hardin, Montana
Bisbee Observer, Bisbee, Arizona
Canadian Record,
   Canadian, Texas
Canyon Country Zephyr,
   Moab and Monticello, Utah
Chadron Record,
   Chadron, Nebraska
Chilkat Valley News,
   Haines, Alaska
Clarion-Ledger,
   Jackson, Mississippi
Concrete Herald,
   Concrete, Washington
Dove Creek Press,
   Dove Creek, Colorado
Dutch Harbor Fisherman,
   Dutch Harbor, Alaska
Freeman South Dakota Courier,
   Freeman, South Dakota
Guadalupe County Communicator,
   Santa Rosa, New Mexico
High Country News,
   Paonia, Colorado
Huntington Advertiser,
   Huntington, West Virginia
Martin Countian, Inez, Kentucky
Martin County Times,
   Inez, Kentucky

Moab Times-Independent,
   Moab, Utah
Mountain Eagle,
   Whitesburg, Kentucky
Neshoba Democrat,
   Philadelphia, Mississippi
Norwood Post,
   Norwood, Colorado
Original Briefs, Hardin, Montana
Rio Grande Sun,
   Espanola, New Mexico
San Juan Record,
   Monticello, Utah
Tabor City Tribune,
   Tabor City, North Carolina
Telluride Daily Planet,
   Telluride, Colorado
Telluride Watch,
   Telluride, Colorado
Tundra Drums,
   Anchorage, Alaska
Unalaska Advertiser,
   Dutch Harbor, Alaska
Vineyard Gazette, Martha's
   Vineyard, Massachusetts
West Valley View,
   Buckeye, Arizona
West Virginia Hillbilly,
   Richwood, West Virginia

WEBSITES

www.canyoncountryzephyr.com
www.dailyyonder.com
www.ruraljournalism.org